The

LODGE SECRETARY

and

DIRECTOR OF CEREMONIES

A Practical Guide

Richard Johnson

Lewis Masonic

Contents

Foreword

Sometimes taking office for the first time can seem a daunting prospect. In this treatise to help the Lodge Secretary and Director of Ceremonies, W Bro Dr Richard Johnson has identified some necessary observations and consequent directions.

The author is to be congratulated on the clarity of this work.

R W Bro John Hale
Provincial Grand Master
Cumberland & Westmorland

Front cover:
Photographs of the Officers' jewels from the Lodge of Peace & Unity 314 in Preston.

First published 2004

ISBN 0 85318 234 5

© Richard Johnson 2004

Published by Lewis Masonic

an imprint of Ian Allan Publishing Ltd, Hersham, Surrey KT12 4RG.
Printed by Ian Allan Printing Ltd, Hersham, Surrey KT12 4RG.

Code: 0401/

Preface

Alexandre Dumas wrote a book called *The Three Musketeers* in 1844. It detailed some of the adventures of Athos, Porthos and Aramis who enjoyed somewhat exalted status in the French Court in the 1620s, and their meeting and befriending of a young newcomer called D'Artagnan, who by joining in some of their exploits was eventually accepted by them and made the three into a quartet.

So what has this to do with a Masonic lodge? Certainly not the swordsmanship and several other aspects of the lives of these 17th Century heroes, but they carried out the private orders of the King and Queen of France, and organised themselves to deliver what was required and within the requested timescale. In the same way it could be said that the Secretary, Director of Ceremonies and Treasurer are the main organisers or components of the "engine room" of any lodge, each often staying in post for several years. D'Artagnan in this case might represent the Master of the lodge, a newcomer to this elevated status (unless the lodge is recycling Past Masters), who is eager to be guided by those with more experience but who may also have quite firm ideas of his own on what could and should be done during his year.

This book forms part of a series concerned with assisting brethren who have taken on different offices within their lodges, the previous books having covered the duties of the Assistant and then the Principal Officers. We now concentrate on the roles of the Secretary and the Director of Ceremonies, leaving the role of the Treasurer and indeed all aspects of monetary matters until a later volume. The Secretary and Director of Ceremonies each have different roles to perform, but their duties tend to dovetail neatly together and cover almost all of the administrative and personnel aspects between them. For the Director of Ceremonies particularly, there will be aspects of his duties that have been partly covered in the advice for the other lodge Officers, and to avoid laboured repetition between the books these aspects have not all been reiterated verbatim in this volume.

For those who have been in post for several years, they will be performing many of the jobs routinely and to the satisfaction of the lodge members – otherwise they would not still be in office, so perhaps this book may be of interest to them essentially as an *aide mémoire*. It has, however, been written mainly for the benefit of the brother

4

who is thinking about or has been invited to become the next Secretary or Director of Ceremonies, and who wishes to learn something about the extent of his new duties. He will doubtless be helpfully briefed by his predecessor before the hand-over, but often it is valuable to be able to absorb quietly some preliminary and practical guidance even before that briefing, so that he has an overall awareness of what will be required, and he can use the briefing to elicit additional information on any remaining areas of concern.

At his investiture, the main duties of the Secretary are outlined in his address as issuing the summons to include all items of business, recording the proceedings as minutes, keeping a register of names and addresses of members, and making the necessary returns to Grand Lodge. The Secretary oversees all of the arrangements for ensuring the lodge is able to function properly, including keeping the lodge records and liaising with the Grand and Provincial Grand Lodge Secretaries as required, as well as the day-to-day organisation of his own lodge meetings and interactions with the local Group, other lodges or the caterers.

The Director of Ceremonies, on the other hand, oversees the physical running of the meetings and practices, and covers all aspects of each participant knowing exactly what to do and when and where. His jurisdiction remains solely within the confines of the lodge, and he only has contact with the outside world when dignitaries come to visit. At his investiture the duties are outlined simply as seeing that "the ceremonies are carried out correctly, all attendees are seated according to status, and the Officers are in place." Rarely can so much responsibility be covered by only 19 words.

So to move away from the swashbuckling activities of the 17th Century, perhaps a more modern analogy for the roles of these two important organisers within the lodge might be found in clubs playing association or rugby football. The Secretary can be viewed as a kind of General Manager, ensuring that there is a stadium booked to play in and that the players, fans and visiting teams and fans know the dates of the fixtures, while the Director of Ceremonies is more like the team Coach, ensuring that each of the players is at peak fitness and totally aware of the appropriate tactics and set pieces for every game. Both roles serve to some extent as backroom staff, however, to ensure that the team participants in every game (or lodge meeting) will be the ones receiving all of the plaudits from the visitors.

And remember that the lodge has requested you personally to undertake either of the two offices. It does not expect you to be a perfect clone of the previous incumbent, indeed it might be hoped that in some ways you perform your duties a little differently, so you do not have to follow exactly the same style as your predecessor. Indeed life would be the poorer if there were no differences between us all, just as one of the pleasures of visiting lodges is to see how each copes with essentially the same Masonic business in a variety of ways. So do not be afraid to bring your own charisma to the job in hand; usefully adopt the best attributes of the person before you, and introduce some new ideas to other aspects of the office, and you will be able to strike an effective balance between continuity and a new broom.

It should be noted that in this book there are repeated references to "Province" and "Group". I am aware that collections of lodges overseas are called "Districts" and are largely equivalent to the UK Provinces, and that some Provinces use the terminology "District" instead of "Group" for a collection of lodges in one locality or under one Assistant Provincial Grand Master for example. It would be appreciated if the reader could bear this in mind if his region adopts one of the other titular options, but this request seems preferable to using Province/District and Group/District throughout and where the different interpretations of "District" may cause confusion. The recent creation of the first Metropolitan Grand Lodge as the London equivalent of a Province, rather than remaining under the direct jurisdiction of the Grand Master, has also served to circumvent the requirement to constantly insert the London equivalent to Provincial protocol where appropriate. Where there are some specific differences between the operations of the District and Metropolitan Grand Lodges and the Provincial Grand Lodges, these are usually commented on as appropriate.

The Secretary will also need to know the contents of the Book of Constitutions – the most up-to-date version and any subsequent booklets with modified sections until the next reprint (currently 2001 plus amendments). In this practical guide there are places where certain regulations in the Book are referred to in the following manner (BoC80). Usefully Grand Lodge tries to keep the paragraph numbering unchanged, even retaining deleted items rather than closing up the numbers. Once you have familiarised yourself with the contents you do not need to alter your memory of the numeracy with every revision, but the sub-paragraphs can change in number and content, so these are not referred to in this guide. And this is not intended to be a complete regurgitation of the Book of Constitutions in another format, as that would be a time-wasting exercise. What is included in the Secretary's section of this guide at the end of each chapter is a listing of some, but not necessarily all, of the rules relevant to aspects of his duties as discussed in the chapter. And the full rules are not reproduced here, but the list only highlights some of the key points covered therein, and although several chapters may refer to the same rule, it is not necessarily repeated at the end of each subsequent chapter. The idea is to guide the new Secretary to areas of the Book where additional explanatory information on the particular subject matter may be found; there is no excuse for skipping your homework and reading the definitive source material for the answers. It is probable that each Master and indeed the whole lodge will be relying on you for detailed advice when it is required, so you have been forewarned even if you are not yet fully prepared.

The Lodge
Secretary

Introduction

"I keep six honest serving-men
(They taught me all I knew);
Their names are What and Why and When
And How and Where and Who."
[Rudyard Kipling, *Just So Stories (1902), The Elephant's Child*]

Both the Secretary and the Director of Ceremonies make use of these serving men. For the Secretary, the lodge has to meet some*where* and on a selected date and time (*when*), conduct a certain agreed amount of business (*what*) involving specified people (*who*) in a recognisable manner (*how*), and it may be required occasionally to explain *why* things have to be the way they are.

The work of the Secretary centres on the lodge and its attendant paperwork. Although the latter will absorb much of the Secretary's time, for any brother contemplating taking on the office he should be aware that a great deal more will be required than merely a copperplate handwriting style for the minutes; this office is the hub of the engine-room of the organisation of the lodge. As Secretary you will be liaising with literally everyone in the lodge on a regular basis and also with many people outside the lodge, because as the record-keeper you are the focus of all formal interactions within and outside the lodge and its members.

Interestingly in the early lodges the Secretary was not a mandatory office, although nowadays the Secretary and Treasurer are denoted as "regular" Officers who must be appointed or confirmed at installations, otherwise the lodge cannot legally function. In those early days the person filling the office had to have received at least a minimal education to be able to read and write, which was not necessarily the case with all of the lodge members. The early Grand Lodges all appointed Grand Secretaries, to exchange correspondence with their lodges and issue *communiqués* to them, and so it was probably not long before lodges appointed their equivalent Officer to act on their behalf. And while the very earliest isolated lodges might have managed with minimal records, once the Grand

Secretaries and Provincial Secretaries began corresponding with lodges, and lodges were visited to check their records were in good order, this Officer had an increasing amount of reading and correspondence to cope with.

At his investiture, the main duties of the Secretary are outlined in his address as issuing the summons for each meeting, recording the minutes of the proceedings, keeping a register of the lodge members, and making the necessary returns to Grand Lodge. This is in fact a useful framework in which to describe the various aspects of the work more fully for a new Secretary, as it covers the meetings, minutes and members of the lodge, and then the external liaisons, leaving only a catch-all to cover any extra items.

The New Secretary

For you to be able to hit the ground running as a newly-appointed Secretary, and it is important that you start well, you will need to have met with the previous Secretary to be fully briefed by him on the organisation of the work involved. You should also have met the Director of Ceremonies and the Master Elect, because those three people will have discussed the anticipated business of the coming 12 months, at least in outline. The retiring Secretary can inform you about the recurring themes in the lodge, such as the business meeting before the installation to ballot for the Master Elect, Treasurer and Tyler as applicable, another lodge meeting traditionally being of limited duration to cater for an Olde English Night, one or two nights with formal visits from local lodges, etc. The Director of Ceremonies and Master Elect can inform you of their particular aspirations for the coming year, including any special events of a one-off nature that they wish to see occur. These might include a talk from a visiting dignitary, a Juniors' or Past Masters' Night, or an evening when several lodge members deliver one or more portions of the lectures associated with the different degrees. And you will hopefully already be aware of any preparations for a member's or the lodge's anniversary – 50th, 100th or whatever.

Another useful prior exercise is for you to read through the Book of Constitutions, and what an educational experience you will find it if you have not already done so. You will doubtless recall that a copy is presented to every Master on his installation with the words: "You will find that there is scarcely a case of difficulty can occur in the Lodge in which that book will not set you right." I wonder how many Masters subsequently gave a second glance to it, preferring instead to be guided by the more senior members of the lodge whenever appropriate. I read the Book of Constitutions several times when we were in the process of founding a new lodge, and drafting the bylaws, etc., and was surprised by just how much information is packed into it, and with a comprehensive index as well. I also have to say that I found the staff in the Grand Secretary's office most helpful when asking for their advice, and also those in the Provincial Secretaries' offices in the Provinces with which I have had most dealings – West and East Lancashire and Cumberland & Westmorland. I am sure that the same applies to the other Provinces, and this helpful support is something that you will come to appreciate during your tenancy of the office of Secretary.

Immediately after having been invested, your first job may be to record the minutes of the installation meeting, and you may be the only one taking notes during the remainder of the meeting. Often the retiring Secretary will have started the minutes for you, leaving some blanks for the numbers of members and visitors and the starting time of the meeting. Otherwise he may hand you his notes of the meeting up until the handover of responsibilities, and leave you to complete the full minutes at your leisure. He may even offer to write up the full minutes as the closing task of his years in office, and your duties then start with the organisation of the next meeting. In this last case, and for ease of future reference, it is probably preferable to keep to the order of the outline of duties as detailed in the address to the Secretary.

Meetings of the Lodge

The Lodge Summons

This is the means by which you inform the members what is planned to happen. There are certain items that have to be included, and certain items that are traditionally included for reference by members or visitors alike. In lodges that have been in existence for some time, the brethren have obviously accepted the house style of the summons, so you should keep to it. Some new Secretaries decide to change the colour, layout or content slightly, and then learn to their cost that no-one else in the lodge wants it that way, even if it saves money, so beware of change for change's sake.

You will have read your lodge summons on many occasions, so it will not be new to you, but spend some time assessing the detail put into the various parts of it, and when they need to be updated. If we first summarise the range of items that can be included in a lodge summons, it will provide a basis for discussing them in more detail later, and you may use it as an *aide mémoire* for your yearly plan of necessary alterations for the lodge meetings. Some lodges have a single-sided sheet for their summons, some adopt a folded double-sided sheet, and others use a loose-leaf insert inside a pre-printed outer cover sheet that is standard for the year. As a basis for discussion we will use the framework of a four-page summons. From perusing a selection of lodge summonses, the following list includes some of the items that may be included:

First Page

Lodge name and number;
Town in which the lodge meets;
Province in which the lodge meets;
Lodge warrant date;
Lodge consecration date;
Lodge logo or picture;
Lodge being the patron of a particular charity or Festival.

Second Page

List of lodge Officers and representatives for the current year;
Addresses and telephone numbers of various lodge Officers;
Address and telephone number of the meeting place;
Contact information of Group Officers;
Almoner to be informed should any member or one of his family be indisposed;
Request for members to inform the Secretary of any change of address;
Reminder to book meals in good time;
Reminder that lodge subscriptions are due;
Statement that Royal Arch is a continuation of the Third Degree and contact names;
Warning that visiting lodges overseas should be referred to Grand Lodge;
Antient Charge about attendance at lodge;
Quote from Dr Oliver about keeping lodge membership select.

Third Page

Sentence from Secretary convening the meeting at the request of the Master, detailing the date, time and place of the meeting;
Secretary's address and telephone number;
Code of dress recommended for the meeting;
Noting any dignitaries who are expected to attend;
Noting at what time the toast to absent brethren will be honoured;
Notice of the dates of practice and committee meetings;
Notice of forthcoming Provincial meeting;
List of business to be transacted at the meeting;
Details of people to be balloted for, and when formally proposed and seconded;
List of brethren due for passing or raising;
List of dates of future lodge meetings;
Statement about meeting happily, etc.

Fourth Page

List of lodge Founders;
List of Past Masters of the lodge;
Annotation of those Founders and Past Masters who have resigned or died;
List of Past Masters of other lodges who are members of the lodge;
List of honorary members of the lodge.

You may be wondering why most lines have been printed in italics; these are the items that are not mandatory for inclusion in a lodge summons, as much of that detail is in other lodge records. It is perhaps surprising how much non-essential information can be and is included, and this list is by no means exhaustive. As stated before, over the years the lodge has grown accustomed to several items of extraneous information being included, as useful reminders for them, and their wishes should obviously continue to be catered for. For visitors, many of these redundant items are interesting for browsing through before and possibly during the meeting, and also if they are bringing greetings from their lodge or are replying to the visitors' toast at the festive board and wish to congratulate a particular Officer on his work.

However, you always have to remember that you need to update much of the information on the summons as required. The regular items such as the date of the meeting should be easy to remember to change, but updating the ranks of brethren as they receive promotion in Grand or Provincial Grand Lodge, or annotating as they resign or die are less regular occurrences and are therefore more likely to be overlooked. It may be useful to try to minimise the changes that have to be made, in order to make your life somewhat easier, but let us first deal with the essentials.

Lodge Name and Number

This uniquely defines the lodge, as it is listed by Grand Lodge (BoC98-9). You may move your lodge, even between Provinces, and the lodge's ranking in the Provincial listings may alter over the years, but the Grand Lodge number stays constant. The regular meeting place and days (i.e. which traditional day in which months) will also appear in the Grand Lodge yearbook, as well as in the Provincial yearbook, and therefore on the first page there is strictly no need for that additional information. On the other hand, decorating the cover page of a four-page summons with biographical details on the start of the lodge, in which Province it currently resides, and a lodge logo or reproduction of the lodge banner is a nice touch, especially for visitors who are with you for the first time as well as for new members. If you temporarily include patronage of the current Provincial Festival charities, then you will need to remember to remove them when no longer required.

Date, Time and Place of Meeting

These are essential for every member and every potential visitor – there is no point in turning up at the wrong date, time or place; the first will change with every meeting, the second may change occasionally (e.g. regular meetings vs. installation meetings), and the third very occasionally. The date is designated in the lodge warrant, unless it has been permanently changed in the interim, in which case the date will be included in the current lodge bylaws (BoC137). And a lodge needs its warrant in order to meet, even with an out-of-date day, so a lost or mislaid warrant will require prompt action to be taken (BoC103). A few lodges still organise their meetings around phases of the moon, which originated when there was no street lighting and the full moon assisted the brethren in their travels to and from the lodge, and these will meet in different weeks of the month; for this they will need a nautical calendar or its equivalent. Some lodges have meetings that clash with Bank Holidays and Christmas, and the variable times that Easter occurs in the year can catch out other lodges that meet on Mondays or Fridays, and a lodge can move its meeting date by up to seven days before or after the designated date with due notification having been sent to the Provincial office. If, however, the lodge wants to move its meeting by more than seven days, then a formal dispensation must be applied for and may require a charge to be paid in advance, and then the dispensation has to be read out in the lodge meeting (BoC139).

Changing the starting time, for example when there is the additional business of the installation of a new Master, does not require approval from Province, although again its office will probably request notification in case they have someone in mind to visit the lodge. The members would probably appreciate having the change of time and date highlighted on the summons, so that several of them do not follow the normal routine for lodge meetings and arrive at the wrong time or on the wrong day.

For special occasions the lodge may wish to meet elsewhere, perhaps for a major lodge anniversary when the expected number of visitors cannot be accommodated in the usual meeting place. Again a formal dispensation must be applied for, and the date and time may be changed as well, and Province also have to check that a regular lodge meeting can be held in the suggested location (BoC141-2). There is therefore the need to give plenty of notice of the lodge's intentions, but it would be unusual if such a major organisational change signalled the start of your secretarial activities – such occasions are normally the subject of meticulous planning over a period of many months.

If the lodge decides to move its normal meeting date and time, and even more so to move its meeting place, then this can take a while liaising with the Provincial and Group Secretaries, and it also requires an approved change of bylaws confirmed formally in lodge for it to be completed (BoC139-42). The early lodges tended to move their meeting places regularly, but they were usually in rented accommodation and were accustomed to testing the landlords' flexibility with menus and prices of meals and drinks in order to obtain the best deals possible, whereas nowadays most lodges meet in Masonic Halls that are owned rather than rented and lodges tend to move around less.

The Essential Business of the Meeting
Many summonses go into great lengths to detail all of the items to be dealt with.

The essential ones which occur on a regular basis are:

To open the lodge;
To confirm the minutes of the previous meeting;
To conduct one or more Craft ceremonies, or to receive a lecture, etc.;
To ballot for various people or Officers;
To transact any other business;
To close the lodge.

For a lodge to conduct any business at all it will have to be formally opened and then closed, so the first and last items are fairly self-explanatory. The opening may include the reading of the summons convening the meeting, which the Secretary may enunciate in full, the delivery of an Antient Charge, and other regular activities, but these do not necessarily have to be noted as separate items on the agenda, although lodges may prefer them to be so. Note that if the Master dies or is incapacitated for a considerable time, the Senior Warden will convene the lodge meetings, and if he is also unavailable it will be the Junior Warden (BoC119).

The confirmation of the minutes is necessary, as it enables members to query or correct any aspect they disagree with in the record of the previous meeting (BoC144). The minutes may be read out in lodge, in which case only the attendees can comment, or may be circulated by post prior to the meeting so that members who cannot attend the next meeting can query aspects of the last meeting they were present at. If the minutes are issued beforehand, it would be a courtesy for the Secretary to be made aware of any reservations that members may have about his minutes, rather than waiting until the lodge meeting. With adequate safeguards on the Internet, it may become more usual for minutes to be e-mailed to members and thereby save on the postage costs. It is becoming more normal for the minutes to be created electronically and in a typed format, so even the previous requirement for a Secretary to have a copperplate handwriting style is of a lower priority than erstwhile. If the brethren do not like the change from handwritten to printed minutes, adopt a script font for them. And even when printed as separate sheets, the minutes have to be fixed into a book as a permanent record.

The ceremonies to be conducted must mention the names of the candidates being processed, for lodge and Provincial record purposes, and there cannot be more than two candidates for any ceremony without prior dispensation from the Provincial Grand Master (BoC168). It is not necessary to detail who will be conducting the different aspects of the ceremonies, although many lodges often choose to designate the major performers. One problem that may arise is the person so named may not be able to attend and someone else will have to fill in for him, but hopefully such glitches are rare and the minutes will in any event record what actually took place at the meeting. Even rarer is that the candidate is not able to attend, but then there will be no ceremony either.

If it is planned that there will be no ceremony, a lecture may be delivered at the meeting. If the speaker is well-known, then it may be of interest to potential visitors to be able to learn who is coming and the title and subject matter of his presentation; although lectures are becoming more common these days, there may be something that attracts people according to their tastes and interests, so be as bullish as you can when the speaker has explained the content of his talk to you. Also if there is no ceremony, there may be the formal presentation of a Grand Lodge Certificate, or a personal or a lodge milestone in Freemasonry, such as a 50th anniversary, or perhaps several members are delivering a section of the Lectures, but there will normally be a main item on the agenda.

The ballots for people – candidates, joining and honorary members – must be included on the summons, together with their details of names, addresses, ages, occupations (full description, not just "Company Director"), membership of other lodges, and proposers and seconders and at which lodge meeting the people's names were first put forward (BoC164). The lodges that use loose-leaf inserts with their summons can accommodate all of this additional information easily, as the size of the insert is not necessarily unchangeable; those with no inserts may decide to use one or to incorporate an extra leaf into their standard summons so that all of the information is contained in the one document.

Any other business can include reports, from the Lodge Committee, Lodge of Instruction, Treasurer, Almoner, Charity Steward, Festival or Group representatives, etc.; propositions and notices of motion; and communications from Grand Lodge, Provincial Grand Lodge, and of a general nature – the risings. Again lodges often want these items to be spelled out in more detail, but that is a lodge preference, and the agenda can be as short as the six items as stated above, or can extend onto two pages if required.

It can be seen that items 1, 2 and 6 do not alter on the summons from meeting to meeting, and item 5 will probably remain unchanged as a catch-all at the end. There may be some aspects that are essentially included in item 5 that have to be expanded into separate items of business from time to time, such as propositions to change subscriptions or bylaws, etc. Item 4 will appear for certain meetings as and when required, such as electing the new Master, but the content of item 3 will change every time, as the main business of each meeting will vary, or else attending lodge will become an extremely boring pastime.

Let us assume that you use the summonses from last year's meetings as a template. You may have regular nights in your calendar for Olde English Night activities or ladies' dining-in nights, when the business of the lodge is traditionally brief; you may have a regular Past Masters' Night to show the juniors how it should be done; you may be blessed with enough juniors to have a regular Juniors' Night, etc., and these are fitted into a traditional sequence of lodge meetings. You begin by pencilling in the standard items of business – opening, minutes, correspondence, closing. You then add the items of business peculiar to the coming meeting and, even if by chance the ceremony is the same as before, it will be performed on a different candidate or will be a demonstration. It may be customary for your lodge summons to show who is undertaking the major roles in the ceremony, and again this will require alteration as the participants change. If the lodge is to receive a talk, you will need to indicate the title and possibly the subject matter so that the brethren are warned what to expect, and you will have to ensure that any Provincial or Grand rank that the speaker has, is correctly indicated.

Two lodge meetings are very different from the rest, and the obvious anomalies are the installation meeting, where you are unlikely to be conducting any additional ceremony, and the previous meeting (often termed the business meeting) when the elections for the ensuing year are held. For this previous meeting, the ballots for the offices of Master, Treasurer and perhaps Tyler must be indicated on the summons. In addition to balloting for these three, the lodge may at the same time confirm or elect its other representatives for the Hall committee, the Group meetings, etc., and all of these items must be included on the agenda (BoC105, 112-5). After his installation, the new Master appoints and invests his Officers (BoC104, 116-7), and perhaps a Past Master's jewel is presented to the outgoing Master.

From time to time there may also be special topics to be covered. The Treasurer may wish to increase the lodge subscriptions (they rarely go in the other direction), and such propositions have to be spelled out in the summons so that the members know what they will be voting on. The Treasurer will also be required to bring the statement of annual accounts before the lodge once each year, duly audited as required. If there is the need to change any aspect of the lodge bylaws, then the new wording has to be written out verbatim. In all likelihood each of these matters will have been thoroughly aired at previous Lodge Committee meetings, which will have determined the exact wording to be used. If any of your Officers die or terminate their services, the Master can appoint or the lodge can elect a replacement accordingly, except that the Master cannot be replaced until the next installation meeting (BoC121).

From time to time your lodge may have to hold an emergency or special meeting, for which the agenda will necessarily be different; there will only be four or possibly five items on it. The lodge will need to open and close as usual, and you will also have to read out the dispensation from Provincial Grand Lodge that has allowed you to call the extra meeting. You then conduct the business of the meeting – the reason why the meeting is taking place. This may be a celebration of a lodge or personal anniversary, or a demonstration ceremony to which you want to invite many more guests than usual, perhaps on a Saturday rather than your usual meeting day. You may also have to hold an emergency ballot if your Treasurer or Tyler is seriously ill, has resigned or died, as the first and possibly the second of these Officers is not appointed by the Master. There will be no other business – not even the confirmation of the minutes of the previous lodge meeting – and the emergency meeting can only transact the business on the agenda (BoC140), so your minutes this time are likely to be brief.

The Non-Essentials on the Lodge Summons

These are the aspects that are likely to catch out the unwary Secretary. You may find it beneficial to compile a master summons that can be changed according to the business of each meeting, noting the many items that do not change frequently. If you are able to create an electronic template, you can then highlight the items that are bound to change – meeting date, main item of business, etc. – with one colour, and perhaps designate those parts of the summons requiring occasional alterations with another colour. Otherwise, Secretaries have found that different highlighter pens can be used on paper to indicate the frequency with which items have to be changed.

As an example, you will already be aware that the summons for the meeting following the installation will have several changes from previous versions. If your summons includes a listing of previous Masters, then for the first meeting after the installation you will need to add a further name (the IPM) to the list. This might also be the time to check that all of the others in the list have their correct ranks designated, unless your lodge summons indicates their ranks only as at their respective installations. Similarly some lodges indicate which Founders or Past Masters of the lodge have resigned or died, and these aspects need to be updated as and when. Also if your summons details the addresses and telephone numbers of any Officers in the lodge, such as the Master, Treasurer, Director of Ceremonies, Almoner, Charity Steward, etc., then these may also need updating – at least the Master's will usually have altered. And don't forget that his name may now be repeated on or near the front of the summons, and if you are a new Secretary then your own name and address should be inserted as the person now notifying the brethren of the next meeting on the new Master's behalf!

There is a lot to remember, and you are perhaps beginning to realise why several lodges have adopted brevity in the summons – it can make the life of a lodge Secretary immeasurably less stressful. In fact many lodges using both sides of the piece of paper try to format one side, the front or the front-and-back cover if folded, that requires no alteration for a year or more. If they list the lodge Founders, they retain their original Grand and Provincial Grand ranks at the consecration rather than repeatedly updating them, and abandon the concept of indicating whether or not they are still members or even alive. With similarly slight adjustments to the standard content of your summons, you can make your future workload significantly simpler.

The Production and Issuing of the Lodge Summons

The first thing you have to establish is what timescale you are working to. You will contact the printer, if you use one, to confirm the deadlines that he can work to in order to produce your summons in time for your mailing to members and outside bodies. This is the time when you appreciate you are on a treadmill. If the lodge meets every month, then you will need to issue a summons every month. Allowing time for printing, collection of the printed copies, inserting them into envelopes, postal delivery, etc., you will soon realise that the master copy may need to be with the printer within a week from the previous meeting. Lesson one: make sure that at that previous meeting you confirm the final details for the next summons, while you have most people together at one time, rather than having to ring round frantically afterwards. In fact many lodges will hand out the summons for the next meeting at their current meeting, and thereby save an appreciable amount of postage, so the planning cycle is then catering for the next-but-one meeting on a regular basis.

You will also need to confirm how the printer wants to operate. He may be happy for you to scribble, legibly, any alterations onto a previous summons or a master summons that you have generated and work off that as a template. In this case he may need to send you a proof copy to confirm he has interpreted your requirements accurately, again using up more time, but definitely necessary. He may be happy if, in these days of personal computers, you send a disc or e-mail of the different new items on the summons for him to insert electronically into the standard layout (assuming computer compatibility), or he may have to scan your hard copy into his system.

One advantage of the loose-leaf insert inside a standard summons for the agenda is that, if you discover you have left off something important, you can rush through a replacement with the offending item(s) of business included; with the more complicated artwork of a summons which has the logo depicted, it may not be so easy to obtain rush copies. If there are ballots or elections, they must be stated on the summons, because every lodge member has to be warned that these decisions are being taken. The inserts cannot be merely handed out at the meeting; they have to be mailed out to the membership so that those who are not regular attendees can decide whether or not to come (BoC164); there are no postal ballots or voting rights *in absentio* at present, decisions are reached by the majority of attendees on the night. If this requires additional postage charges, so be it; there have been occasions when details have been left off a summons and the ballot for a candidate or even the vote to sponsor a daughter lodge have not been held because of their omission.

You will then have to send out the summons and any other literature to be included – perhaps a newsletter from Grand Lodge or a flyer for a forthcoming lodge function – to all of the members plus several others. A helpful printer may agree to address a set of envelopes for you from a standard list, so that all you have to do is insert the contents and seal them in; otherwise he may run off a set of address labels for you to use. In this day and age, take advantage of modern technology – there is no point in laboriously handwriting all of the envelopes every month, even if our ancient brethren did so, and there are probably many other things you could be profitably devoting your time to instead. And you should not include any Masonic designations on the envelopes, and also do not use postcards for any Masonic communication.

With regard to the mailing list and the number of copies of the summons to order, you need obviously to include every member of the lodge. Province will advise you of additional copies it requires, and certainly the Provincial Secretary will need a copy, while it may be customary to distribute a copy to each local lodge as well as to the Group Officers. If several lodges meet in one Hall, you will need to insert a summons into each appropriate pigeonhole, otherwise add the relevant names and addresses to your list. And remember to print a few spare copies of the summons for visitors who arrive unannounced; it always seems slightly discourteous to have run out of copies when anybody at the meeting requests one, and a few extra copies cost very little – the main cost is setting up for the first copy. If, however, you are running out of copies of the summons before the start of the meeting, also remember to keep one back for inclusion in the Minute Book (preferably leave it at home), and another three for the Principal Officers if you usually place one on each of their pedestals.

Practice and Lodge Committee Meetings

Assuming that you are inheriting the secretarial duties of an established lodge, you are expected to continue the routine without significant change. If your accommodation is shared with other lodges, or has outside lets in order to create an income stream, you will need to ensure that all of the meetings your lodge wishes to hold during the year are booked well in advance. These will include the formal lodge meetings, practice meetings and Lodge Committee meetings, and if there are several rooms to choose from, you will need to book the larger rooms for your bigger meetings such as the installation. It will be your duty as Secretary to ensure that all the regular booking slots are retained for your lodge, and at some time in the year the Hall diary will be available for entering your requirements over the next year. Hopefully your predecessor will have given you a good start by pre-booking as much as he can, but make yourself aware of when the new diary comes out.

Remember that the lodge will have practice meetings between the lodge meetings, and extra practices may be required for major occasions such as installations, while some lodges will also have Lodges of Instruction attached to them. Lodges of Instruction are much more formally organised under the jurisdiction of the lodge, with its Officers being appointed and minutes of the meetings taken (BoC132-5). The Lodge Committee meetings are sometimes organised separately from the practice meetings, in which case they do not have to meet in the lodge room if there is a smaller room available. Most lodges prefer to have regular dates for these additional meetings, so that all of their members establish a constant routine during the Masonic season and have less chance of forgetting where they should be. In the larger Halls remember there might be other side degrees which also have regular meeting dates, and this can inhibit lodges that wish to vary their practice meeting dates.

Once a year you may have a Past Masters' meeting, when the experienced members meet for an overall assessment of the lodge. The topics may include discussing not just the next Master but also looking a few years ahead, assessing how the juniors are performing, recommending which members can be put forward for Provincial honours or promotions, and reviewing the finances of the lodge in general. This will normally be held some time before the installation meeting, and may traditionally include a meal with the Wardens designate of the lodge – they might learn a great deal from listening to the opinions of the senior lodge members about them and their colleagues! If you are a Past Master you will know all about this meeting, but if you are a junior then you may not, and the outgoing Secretary should brief you on the normal arrangements and perhaps invite you to the meeting to see what happens before you take over.

Aspects of the Rules (concerning Meetings)
BoC98-99 – the lodge name, approved by Grand Lodge, and the number, given by Grand Lodge and ranked accordingly in precedence, are as stipulated on the warrant, and only the Grand Master can approve a change of name or title.

BoC103 – if the lodge warrant is lost, the lodge must suspend meetings unless a letter from Grand Lodge authorises the continuance of meetings until a warrant of confirmation is supplied by the Grand Master.

BoC104 – the nine regular Officers of the lodge are the Master, Senior and Junior

Wardens, Treasurer, Secretary, Senior and Junior Deacons, Inner Guard and Tyler; no person can hold two regular offices at the same time.

Of the eight additional Officers, two shall be appointed: Almoner and Charity Steward, and the other six may be appointed: Chaplain, Director of Ceremonies and his Assistant, Organist, Assistant Secretary, and Steward(s); a regular Officer can also hold one additional office.

Of the 17 named Officers, only the Tyler may be a non-member of the lodge; the lodge may deem the Secretary's services are equivalent to his subscription, but it still has to pay his Grand Lodge and Provincial Grand Lodge dues; all Officers are appointed by the Master except the Treasurer and Tyler (if a non-member) and himself, who all have to be elected.

BoC105 – the Master Elect is elected at the meeting before the installation.

BoC107 – if the notice that the Master Elect cannot be installed is less than seven days before the installation meeting, the current Master continues for another year.

BoC112-3 – the Treasurer and Tyler (if applicable) shall be elected at the same meeting as the Master Elect.

BoC115 – a Master cannot remain in office for more than two consecutive years except by dispensation from the Provincial Grand Master; nor can a person be the Master of two or more lodges at the same time except by dispensation from the Grand Master for Metropolitan Areas and Provinces, or from the District Grand Master overseas.

BoC116 – the Master appoints appropriately and invests all Officers at the installation meeting.

BoC117 – the proprietor or manager of the meeting place of the lodge cannot be an Officer of that lodge except by dispensation from the Provincial Grand Master.

BoC119 – if the Master is incapacitated, removed, resigns or dies, the Senior Warden calls the meetings, or in his absence the Junior Warden does so; the IPM or another Installed Master shall occupy the Master's chair and confer degrees, but if the Master's absence is temporary he may nominate a member who is an Installed Master to rule the lodge during his absence.

BoC121 – any regular Officer, except the Master, can be replaced for the remainder of the year by appointment or election as appropriate.

BoC132-5 – the times and places of meeting of Lodges of Instruction shall be submitted for approval to the Provincial Grand Secretary, minutes of the meetings shall be kept, and brethren appointed to office.

BoC137 – lodge bylaws shall specify the regular meeting days and place of the lodge, and the regular meeting for the elections and the subsequent installation meeting.

BoC139 – no lodge meeting shall be held on Christmas Day, Good Friday or a

Sunday, but may be held on a Bank Holiday; if the lodge meeting falls on one of those days (including Bank Holidays) the lodge can move its meeting by ±7 days without dispensation; the lodge may move its meeting for any reason by ±28 days only with a dispensation from the Provincial Grand Master.

BoC140 – the lodge may hold an emergency meeting, called only by the senior available Principal Officer, by dispensation from the Provincial Grand Master; the business conducted must be limited to that on the summons for the meeting, and the minutes of the previous regular lodge meeting shall not be confirmed.

BoC142 – if it is impracticable or undesirable for a lodge to hold any meeting at its regular place, the Master shall apply to the Provincial Grand Master for a dispensation to meet elsewhere.

BoC144 – a Minute Book shall record that the minutes of the previous meeting were confirmed at the subsequent regular lodge meeting.

BoC163 – the necessary details of joining, rejoining and initiation candidates shall be included on or with the summons for the lodge meeting at which their ballot will take place.

BoC164 – the candidate's particulars and the Master's certificate shall be read out prior to the ballot for membership; the summons with the details of the candidate(s) shall be sent to all lodge members no less than 10 days before the meeting.

BoC165 – three black balls in the ballot shall reject the candidate, or less if so stated in the lodge bylaws, and the candidacy cannot be re-submitted until a reasonable period shall have elapsed, which may be quantified in the lodge bylaws.

BoC168 – there shall not be more than two candidates for any ceremony worked in the lodge without dispensation from the Provincial Grand Master.

Minutes of the Lodge

Preparing for the Lodge Meeting

The best method of operating as Secretary at a lodge meeting is to be well prepared. If you are not an organised person, you may have to work hard at this, but after some flustered moments in your first few meetings you will rapidly realise that you should have gathered everything you need into the correct running order as laid out in your agenda, so that you have the right piece of paper at the right time.

Arriving at the meeting place in good time, you will first place the signature or attendance (Tyler's) book or sheets at the entrance to the lodge room, for members and visitors to sign, and visitors must be vouched for by the members (BoC125). This is your method of recording who was present at every meeting, and although the Tyler has jurisdiction of the paperwork while it is outside the door of the lodge, you will claim possession of it afterwards in order to insert at least the numbers attending into your minutes, and if sheets they will need to be affixed into a permanent record. You will also place any spare copies of the summons near the entrance, or on your table if that is the norm, as well as perhaps placing copies for the Principal Officers and the Director of Ceremonies as appropriate. If you have dignitaries attending, you might also keep some copies for them as well, even if you have already posted each a copy, in case some have forgotten to bring theirs with them.

You will also set out your own items as required. You will need the lodge Minute Book with the minutes of the previous meeting completed and ready for signature. You will need a notebook for recording aspects of the current meeting, or if you have planned ahead you may have already compiled a skeletal framework into which to enter the details. Again with computers, it is comparatively easy to produce an individualised running order for each meeting, to help minimise the writing you have to do. For example, you should know who is making a planned proposition and who is seconding it, so you are only awaiting any additional items that are sprung on you. Similarly you will have already compiled a list of apologies for absence to be read out, and you will only need to note those added personally by brethren at the meeting. Essentially the minutes will follow the agenda on the summons, but highlighting any differences that occurred from the planned activities: some Officers were not present and were substituted by other members, the candidate or the lecturer could not attend and perhaps another lecture was given, etc.

Your desk may also have to cater for any additional items required by the lodge, such as ballot boxes, balls and slips of paper if there are any ballots to be taken, and bags or plates for the charity collection. For an initiation ceremony there is the need to provide a copy of the lodge bylaws and an up-to-date Book of Constitutions to be presented to the candidate. If your lodge presents copies of the Peterborough booklets after each ceremony, you will need these for the candidates, and also a copy of the Emulation or the lodge ritual book if you present one to each new Master Mason. Some time after the raising there should be his Grand Lodge certificate to be presented.

Conducting the Lodge Meeting

When the meeting starts you have a dual role, that of replying when called on by the Master, and that of recording what transpires. You will be on your feet several times to cover various matters, and it is now apparent how important it is that you have organised your information in a logical order which parallels the business you have listed on the summons. This preparation is well worthwhile; you may have seen several Secretaries fumbling for pieces of information that they know they have brought to the meeting, but which have been temporarily mislaid, and it does not indicate a great deal of efficiency.

You will need to record the presence of any visiting dignitaries, some of whom can demand admission into the lodge room rather than be invited in by the Master (BoC122-4). They will not only sign the Tyler's book or sheet, but will probably also receive a formal salute depending on their rank and, if they are sufficiently senior, they will be accompanied by the Provincial Director of Ceremonies or one of his Deputies and whose presence should also be noted.

The method of approving the minutes will vary from lodge to lodge (BoC144). In the olden days the minutes were entered into a Minute Book and required reading out loud in lodge at the next meeting. If your lodge still reads out the minutes at each meeting, you or perhaps the Assistant Secretary may perform the task. In these days of computers and photocopying, many lodges post a copy of the minutes to each member, and the Master can then simply ask for a vote on the acceptability of the minutes as circulated without taking up lodge time in having them read. It should be noted that as yet lodges are not entrusting their minutes solely in an electronic format, but are required to print off a hard copy to be retained in the lodge records. Grand Lodge insists that the printed minutes are affixed to the pages of a bound Minute Book. If you are considering sending any information, minutes or otherwise, by the Internet, be warned about the restrictions concerning the publishing of Masonic proceedings (BoC177). There are relatively new IT and Internet lodges around the country which can advise you on the latest labour- and time-saving methods currently allowed by the different Provinces.

After the minutes have been accepted and signed, which may require you or the Deacons carrying them to the Master and Wardens as appropriate, you may be then called upon to report any apologies for absence. If any Officers are not able to be present, this gives the Master the opportunity to thank the substitutes for standing in for their colleagues, but in some lodges apologies are given later under the risings.

There may then be a ballot for candidates, whether joining members, honorary members or prospective initiates. It should be noted that a single ballot can be held for multiple candidates, but if there are too many negative votes on the first round, then the ballot is split into the separate parts and repeated to confirm where the problem lies, if there is one (BoC165). You may be required to read out the details you have entered into the summons, or be allowed to state that full details are printed thereon, but you will have to read out the Master's declaration certifying that each one is a fit and proper person to be admitted as a member of the lodge (BoC164). If the ballot takes place at your table you may be involved, or the Deacons may take the ballot box from your desk and issue the ballot balls to and collect from the lodge members.

Whether the decision is unanimous or not, you will record that the ballot was successful if that is the case; to sometimes record a unanimous vote and not at other times may cause potential embarrassment to a candidate and his proposer and seconder in the latter instance. Should the votes in a show of hands be evenly cast, the Master has a second casting vote (BoC156). If the vote is adverse, you will have to record the fact and later inform the candidate of the result. The candidate's sponsors may want to know how long they must wait if they want to re-propose him, obviously after trying to clear up any misconceptions some members may have about him, and you can advise them that it should be some time before they try again (BoC165 states a reasonable period – your lodge bylaws may quantify that as six months, one year or whatever). There should hopefully never be an adverse ballot, if lodge members have voiced their concerns about any candidate to the proposer and seconder, but some lodges insist on balloting for a candidate for initiation at a meeting some time before the ceremony, in order to avoid ever having a candidate waiting outside who has to be told the ceremony is deferred.

Some Masters will ask whether or not a mistake has been made if the ballot is not in favour, but this should be done with care – each member is free to vote with his conscience in private and should not be called to account. However, sometimes there are newly initiated members who are not sure of the correct procedure, and I have attended meetings where the question has allowed them to apologise for inadvertently voting incorrectly without any rancour. A word of warning: if the Master has not spelled out the correct procedure for voting and there are relatively new members present, then you as Secretary should volunteer to remind the members how to vote, hopefully before any mistakes occur – you are part of the Master's supporting team.

If the ballot is happily successful, you will need to retire from the lodge if you require any final signatures from the candidate for initiation before he enters the lodge room. The Treasurer may accompany you if it is the custom in your lodge to relieve the candidate of his cheque for the initiation fee only after the ballot has taken place, and in that case you will both re-enter the lodge to report that the business has been satisfactorily transacted.

The next item of business will then be the ceremony, whether initiation, passing or raising, and unless you are participating you can sit back and enjoy it. You should be aware of who is performing each part of the ceremony, so you are only confirming the meeting runs according to plan. You or the Assistant Secretary may be the official prompter if required, so you should perhaps still be following the ceremony closely; this is not the time to be shuffling papers around your desk. If there is a talk being given by a lodge member or a visitor, then you need to decide in what detail you will record it. To merely record the title is probably insufficient, and if you can obtain a copy of the talk, then you can append it to the minutes so that others can peruse the detail if required. However, several speakers will not bring a written script or printed copy for you, and you therefore need to listen to the talk and perhaps highlight the salient points covered, and possibly record some of the questions asked afterwards by the attendees if any are posed. If a member of the lodge formally thanks the speaker, then this also should be noted.

An installation cannot proceed if the Master Elect is not present (BoC108), unless he is an installed Master continuing for a second year, in which case a simple declaration will suffice. If the Master Elect has died or is not able to be installed, and the lodge has more than seven days notice before the installation, it can call another meeting and ballot for a new Master Elect and install him at the following meeting; if less than seven days, the existing Master has to continue for a second year (BoC106). If a new Junior Warden is not present to be invested at the installation, he will not have served a full year in office, and cannot be considered for the next Master Elect, except by dispensation from the Provincial Grand Master (BoC109); if he is present at the next installation and invested as Senior Warden, then there is no problem.

Thereafter in the meeting that follows there is a series of short items of business which can be briefly recorded. These may include a collection for Masonic charities and receiving an Almoner's report on the well-being of the members (hopefully you will receive some written notes from the Almoner if he has a lot to cover and you want to record the main concerns), and then may come propositions and notices of motion. You will have a running order of who will be proposing and seconding each item, or you will have delegated someone to do so on behalf of any absentees, so the Master may ask you to invite the brethren to speak out in turn. If a proposition is seconded and then an amendment is proposed and seconded, the amendment must be voted on first. If the amendment is successful, it stands; if unsuccessful, then the initial proposition is voted on and the result fully recorded. Your preparation should have ensured that everything that occurs in lodge is following your schedule, so you should not have to note any changes unless someone has his apologies for absence tendered by a colleague on the night, or someone makes a formal complaint about the lodge proceedings (BoC155).

After any other business there are the risings, when you report on communications from Grand Lodge, Provincial Grand Lodge, and of a general nature. It makes for efficiency if you have put all of this correspondence in the order you wish to report it, and possibly only elaborate on the full details if so instructed in that correspondence. The Master will then conduct the closing of the lodge, with you noting the time of completion just as you did the time of starting the meeting. The final record you may add, if it is your lodge tradition, is the amount of money raised in the charity and/or any other collections, both in the lodge room and at the festive board.

Recording the Lodge Meeting
When you write up the minutes is down to you. Some Secretaries like to complete their minutes while the meeting is still fresh in their minds, but others prefer to leave it for a few days. If you have a monthly cycle of lodge meetings, and you send every member a copy of the minutes, then you will have the same deadline as finalising and printing the summons; it seems a waste of lodge funds to send out two missives where one envelope can contain both items. If you have a tight deadline, then you can appreciate the benefit of having reasonably terse minutes rather than the overly flowery and detailed kind. Having said that, the first minutes you complete as a new Secretary, if they are of the installation meeting, will necessarily be lengthy because they will include the people taking part in the ceremony as well as the complete listing of new Officers invested by the Master.

To read the minutes of some of the early lodges is quite revealing. Often the handwriting was immaculate and is easily legible even now, and possibly it was necessary to write clearly if you were later trying to read out your own minutes by glimmering candlelight. Also the reviews of the meeting could be very brief, without some of the embellishments used today. Several entries would summarise the meeting as being opened at W o'clock with X members present and perhaps all of their names listed as Officers; Brother Y being initiated, passed or raised; and the lodge being closed in harmony at Z o'clock. It was assumed that each lodge Officer performed his duty according to the requirements of the office and the traditions of the lodge. Sometimes the names of the few if any visitors would be noted, but other items were deemed to be superfluous. Perhaps if the Secretary found writing a difficult chore it was understandable that the minutes were short, but they gave little extra detail away, except at the installations when the new Officers were recorded. Also it should be noted that several older lodges used to meet every fortnight, and with such a short time between meetings it is not surprising that some of the Secretaries were somewhat frugal with the contents of their minutes.

This may be a useful time to comment on the detail you might wish to include. There are some Secretaries who think that every detail should be recorded: "Brother A stood, turned to salute the Worshipful Master, turned back to the candidate, cleared his throat, smiled, and spoke in a firm but reassuring manner…" They will also comment on the capability of the brother in performing his task, and have a range of adjectives for almost every occasion. After listening to or reading several minutes of this type, you realise that some Secretaries must be constantly referring to *Roget's Thesaurus* to pay a compliment but avoiding the re-use of the same adjectives all the time, and you also learn of the fine gradation and nuances of the adjectives chosen to comment on the quality of the work in lodge from first class to acceptable. At the next meeting those minutes bring the ceremony alive in great detail to all the attendees of the event, but does it matter thereafter?

The lodge minutes are supposed to be a record for posterity, and that amount of detail will only fill the Minute Books with remarkable rapidity, and take an undue amount of time in reading the minutes at each meeting. The minutes can record the bare minimum, paralleling the concept of limiting the summons to the essentials if required. In this sense to record that the "candidate was initiated by the Master and his Officers" should suffice in most cases. You do not have to include that the candidate was admitted into the lodge room by the Inner Guard (it's his job), conducted by the Junior Deacon (it's his job), presented by the Senior Warden (it's his job), obligated by the Master (it's his job), etc. What is important is if the proposer has stood in as Junior Deacon in order to conduct his candidate through his first ceremony, and his seconder was invited by the Master to occupy the chair of King Solomon to obligate his candidate, then these facts should be recorded. In a similar vein a full list of lodge Officers does not necessarily have to be written down at every meeting, as they will probably be listed in the summons for the meeting or whilst being appointed at the previous installation, but any substitutes for absent Officers should be noted.

Another way of regarding the lodge records is that they should perhaps also highlight any departures from the norm, in the same way that you may drive down a stretch of motorway every day, but after three months you will only remember the journeys when something unusual has happened. A meeting of one lodge recently started a little late because England was playing Belgium in the 2002 World Cup and most of the members and virtually all of the guests were in various local hostelries watching the match live on television. England managed to win 3-0, and as these happy occurrences are not guaranteed even every four years, the Secretary noted the reason for the tardiness in opening the lodge. In several Preston lodge minutes surprisingly little mention was made of the outbreak of or the happenings during the First or Second World Wars, except for apologies and some lodges sending food hampers to prisoners. One lodge did note that an Army officer had tried to requisition the lodge room in the middle of a meeting to bivouac his troops – it would have been interesting to learn exactly how the Tyler with only a sword kept off a regiment with rifles, bayonets, mortars, etc., or perhaps it might have been the provision of a round of drinks that bought the required time to finish the meeting. In the Second World War a couple of lodge meetings were interrupted by air raid sirens, but the lodges managed to complete the ceremonies even after over half of the Officers had had to leave in order to perform their wartime duties.

These additional entries might also include comments at the meeting from a visitor to the Master whilst tendering greetings or to/from a dignitary whilst being welcomed into the lodge. At one installation the Master offered the gavel of the lodge to the visiting Assistant Provincial Grand Master, as he was bound to do, with the warning that the handle was coated in super-glue, but the quick-thinking visitor managed to avoid a potentially sticky situation by taking hold of the head of the gavel and then returning the implement handle-first with alacrity. On another occasion a lodge member addressed the Master as "Worshipful Mother", a fact gleefully noted in the minutes and in the subsequent lodge history. There is nothing wrong with enjoying our meetings, and passing on aspects of that enjoyment to others, is there?

Recording the Lodge Committee Meeting
In many ways the Lodge Committee meeting – and the business forum of your lodge may have a different name – parallels the lodge meeting, but without the ceremonies or lectures. Just as the lodge meeting operates with an agenda of items of business, so should the committee meeting. If there is one already, then use it at

each meeting, and if one does not yet exist, then you might consider creating one. It provides a useful framework for the Master to operate within, and at his first Lodge Committee meeting he will be grateful for such assistance.

The Lodge Committee can usefully deal with and make decisions on many items of business, without the need to repeat them all again in open lodge, although some of the deliberations will need to be reported formally in lodge. The Lodge Committee meeting enables the members to discuss items, possibly contentious ones, *in camera* before communicating the agreed decision in lodge when visitors are present. Of course the Master has the power *in extremis* to ask the visitors to leave a lodge meeting before it is closed (or delay its opening) so that lodge members can discuss domestic items privately, but most lodges prefer not to leave their guests unattended in this way.

The first items of business are usually to note those present and accept apologies for absence, and then to read the minutes of the previous meeting, or the minutes can be circulated to members in order to avoid this loss of time. Then come the matters arising, when members report on actions they have undertaken and responses they have received. It is important that all aspects of the matters arising are reported, closed or are continuing, and it is useful for you or the Master to summarise the conclusions reached, the results of any votes taken and further actions placed. It is also better to allow actions to run only for a few meetings rather than lingering on the minutes for several months without any perceptible result and by which time the initial intention is almost forgotten; in such cases suggest closing the action and placing a new one.

It is probable that correspondence will be taken next, and there may be several discussions arising from different communications emanating from Grand Lodge and Province. There will also be requests from Masonic and other bodies for donations from the lodge, but it may sometimes make a bigger impact if lodges decide to make a joint contribution to a local charity, so it may be wise to discuss the possibilities with your fellow lodges as appropriate. The Lodge Committee is a useful occasion to cover some of the more trivial correspondence, leaving only the more important items to be reported formally in the lodge meeting.

There may then be reports from various lodge representatives of meetings and other subjects they need to cover. These can include attendance at the committee meetings convened by the Masonic Hall, the local Group of lodges, or the Province, and there may be several actions cascading down from these bodies, often with certain monetary demands on lodges such as the Hall fees for meetings and other events. Having touched on money matters, the Treasurer and Charity Steward may also offer a review of how the lodge is operating. The lodge subscriptions should be kept under constant review, as expenses always seem to rise, and the Lodge

Committee will be the first to discuss how the subscriptions should be levied in the future. The Charity Steward may need to report on general matters or a Festival if one is currently ongoing in the Province, and he will always be ready to suggest how he can relieve lodge members of money for good causes. The Almoner may also need to acquaint lodge members of any problems that he sees in an individual's circumstances, but only in general terms; the details should necessarily remain confidential.

Next may be a review of the imminent lodge meeting and any changes in the team of Officers and brethren participating. The Lodge Committee meeting may take place immediately after a lodge practice, so the Director of Ceremonies should already know that the team is in good shape. It may be prudent to look further ahead by one or two additional meetings, to ensure that there is consensus about the future business of the lodge. There may be special meetings envisaged, such as a visiting lodge demonstrating a ceremony from another Masonic Constitution, and these will take more planning and effort than the usual lodge meeting, especially as this requires permission from Grand Lodge via the Provincial Secretary.

If your lodge is large in numbers and has a vibrant social life, there may be a social committee in existence, consisting of at least a social secretary and treasurer. They will report on plans for future events, and occasions such as Ladies' Evenings which may require the venue to be booked several months in advance. Even events such as Olde English Nights and Burns' Suppers take a degree of planning, and can often involve the younger and more enthusiastic lodge members in their organisation, which can give them an insight into some aspects of how the lodge operates. If your lodge is smaller, then you may be discussing how to arrange social events that can be shared with other lodges rather than struggling on alone, and a fuller attendance at a joint function may be preferable to a small lodge bouncing around in a large room with acres of space.

Also in smaller lodges there may be discussions about the overall future of the lodge, including amalgamations with other lodges, or even handing in the lodge warrant completely. In this case it is necessary to ensure that every member has the opportunity to express his feelings on the matter. This does not mean that all statements have to be written down verbatim, but certainly a general consensus and any vote taken on a future course of action should be recorded, together with the main arguments for and against being briefly noted. The consensus may alter with time as the perception of the problem changes, but the minutes should be able to define how and after what deliberations any decision was reached.

Aspects of the Rules (concerning Minutes)

BoC106 – if through death or other cause the Master Elect cannot become Master with notice of seven or more days before his would-be installation, an emergency meeting shall be called to ballot for a new Master Elect, and he shall be installed instead.

BoC108 – if the Master Elect is not present at the installation, the meeting shall be postponed for not more than five weeks, and if he still cannot be present the current Master continues for another year, appointing his Officers at the postponed meeting when it takes place.

BoC109 – if a newly selected Warden misses the installation he is deemed not to have held the office for a full year, and is ineligible for immediate election as Master Elect, except by dispensation from the Provincial Grand Master; if he serves as both Junior and Senior Warden but misses one installation, there is no problem.

BoC122 – The Grand Master, Pro Grand Master, Deputy Grand Master and Assistant Grand Master can demand admission into any lodge and must be offered the gavel of the lodge; the Provincial Grand Master and his Deputy or Assistant can demand the same in his own Province.

BoC123-4 – The Grand Master may command any of his Grand Officers to visit any lodge, and the Provincial Grand Master may command any of his Provincial Officers to visit any lodge in his Province, and his representative will be seated on the immediate right of the Master's chair.

BoC125 – every visitor shall be vouched for by a member of the lodge, or allowed entrance into the lodge after due examination, production of his Grand Lodge Certificate and proof of good standing in his own lodge and, if from another Constitution, it must be one that is recognised by Grand Lodge (check such recognition with the Provincial Secretary); the Master has ultimate responsibility for allowing any non-member into his lodge.

BoC144 – a Minute Book shall contain the details of all ceremonies, ballots and elections held in the lodge, and the personal details of all candidates to become members of the lodge, joining or initiates; all persons present at lodge meetings; and a record that the minutes of the previous meeting were confirmed at the subsequent meeting.

BoC155 – every lodge can regulate itself within the general laws and regulations of the Craft, but any protest by a brother concerning consistency with those laws has to be minuted when it is so requested.

BoC156 – when the votes are equal and a majority decision is required, the Master, or Warden when ruling the lodge in his stead, shall have a second vote.

BoC177 – the proceedings of a lodge shall not be published without the consent of the Provincial Grand Master.

Appendix

Examples of Lodge Minutes

There are many and varied styles to writing the lodge minutes, the length of which can vary as the Secretaries change. In the early days of Masonry the minutes tended to be brief and to record only the essentials of the meeting. Apart from listing the Officers, members and (sometimes) visitors present, and noting the date and place of the meeting, they could cover the business with only a few lines in the Minute Book. Even in the Victorian era, although the minutes became more structured, they could still be only slightly longer.

Lodge of Peace and Unity 314 (1797), period 1797-8

The lodge was opened in the First Degree of Masonry when one candidate came forward, and Daniel McKenzie (was admitted) to that degree of an Entered Apprentice. Secondly the lodge was further opened in the Fellowcraft, when Bro Gilgower and Bro McKenzie received the same degree; the night spent in harmony, the following brethren being present (9 members).

The lodge was opened in the First and Second Degrees of Masonry, when four candidates came forward – John Winstanley, William Stockdale, Daniel Arkwright and James Mayor received the degrees of an Entered Apprentice and Fellowcraft; a lecture given by the W Master, several songs by the brethren, the night spent in harmony; the following brethren were present (12 members and visitor, Bro. Addison).

(Night of Emergency) The lodge was opened in the Third Degree of Masonry, when ten candidates came forward to that sublime degree of a Master Mason – Bros. Gilgower, Huggin, Jackman, Irvin, Westmore, Stockdale, Winstanley, Arkwright, Mayor, Ainsworth. The lodge closed in harmony – the following brethren were present (5 members).

Being the Anniversary of St. John the Evangelist the lodge was opened in the First, Second and Third Degrees of Masonry when the following brethren were elected Officers for the ensuing half-year and were obligated and took their chairs in due form. The lodge was closed in harmony (list of 8 Officers and 3 visitors, Bros. Wright, Longmires and Miller).

Lodge of Unanimity 113 (1812), period 1814-16; originally a military Antient lodge of the Third Royal Lancashire Militia

The lodge opened at 4 o'clock in the 3rd Degree for the purpose of installing the Officers that were to be installed for the 6 months ensuing and also for the purpose of celebrating the Festival of St John, when Bro. Broughton was installed W.M., Bro. Grundy S.W., Bro. Kenyon was appointed J.W. for the time being or during the indisposition of Bro. Birtwistle, Bro. Miller was appointed Secretary, Brother Clark Treasurer, Bro. Hawksworth S.D., Bro. Waddington J.D., Bro. Thompson Tyler. Brothers Clark, Plant, Waddington, Cookson, Green, Nicholson and Davis were reappointed as a committee. Visiting Brothers, Whittaker, Lodge 306 and Worsley, No. 888. The lodge was opened in harmony and closed in love at 11 o'clock.

The lodge opened at 1/2 past 5 o'clock in the 3rd Degree for the furtherance of business, when Brother John Brereton W.M. was on the throne, and the rest of the Officers and brothers in their respective places, when Brother Nicholson received the Degree of P Master and the W.M. read the by-laws for the regulation of the members. Visiting Brothers Patterson, W.M. 303, Ingels, S.W. 303, Hughs 303, Breathwite 303. The lodge opened in harmony and closed in love at 1/2 past 8 o'clock.

Lodge No. 179 opened an Entered Apprentice Lodge, for the purpose of collecting monthly dues and delivering the following certificates to Brothers George Green, John Cookson, James Marsden and Thomas Glover when they withdrew their G. Lodge certificates being discharged from the regiment; the W. Master in the Chair and the rest of the Officers and members in their respective places. Having finished the business, the lodge closed in love and harmony.

Lodge of Silent Temple 126 (1760), period 1816-20

Opened on the first Degree. Peter Bolland was proposed by Bro. G. Brown, deposit £1.1.0.

Opened on the first Degree and Peter Bolland was regularly made an Entd. Apprentice Mason. Peter Bolland paid £2.2.0.

Opened on the first Degree and Peter Bolland proposed to take the 2nd Degree; visitor, Thomas Heap from Accrington.

Brother G. Hodgson raised to a Master Mason. Bro. Peter Bolland passed to Fellow Craft. Charles Duckworth was balloted in Master for the ensuing year; visitor, George Maxwell.

Brother Peter Bolland proposed to be raised to Master Mason. One pound to be given to Abram Riley and one pound to be given to Wm. Dent.

Brother Peter Bolland raised to a Master Mason; 2 visitors, John Sutcliffe and George Maxwell.

It was agreed that £1 to be given to Bro. A. Riley and £1 to Wm. Dent. Opened in the 3rd Degree and not any business done, being the annual meeting; Charles Duckworth new Master, W Yates S.W., W Lister J.W., H Brady Inner Guard, J Worswick Tyler, H Ashworth Secretary, J Halstead Sen. Deacon, J Clegg Jun. Deacon, R Raw Steward and T Binns Steward; 2 visitors from Preston (unnamed).

Lodge of the Three Grand Principles 441 (1836), period 1862

(following list of attendees: Officers, members and visitors)

The lodge was opened in due form in the 1st Degree.
The minutes of the last meeting were read and confirmed.
The lodge was opened in the 2nd Degree when James Banham (having previously answered the probationary Questions) was passed to the Degree of a F.C.
The W.M. proposed and the Secretary seconded Mr Baldwin Latham, Secretary to the Board of Health Ely, as a fit and proper person to be made a Mason.
The lodge was then closed in due and ancient form.

The lodge was opened in form in the 1st Degree and the minutes of the last meeting were read and confirmed.
Mr Baldwin Latham was balloted for and unanimously elected.
The lodge was opened in the 2nd Degree. The lodge was opened in the 3rd Degree and Bro. James Banham was raised to the Sublime Degree of a M. M. The lodge was then closed in the 3rd and 2nd Degrees.
On the motion of the S.D. seconded by Bro. Secretary 40 votes were awarded to Bro. Beckett. On the motion of Bro. Wells seconded by the J.W. 4 votes were awarded to Alice Yeates on application on the widows' assistance fund.
The lodge was then closed in due and ancient form.

In the late 19th and in the 20th Centuries many minutes recorded the lodge business in minute detail, although some Secretaries managed to remind attendees of what took place at the meeting, and intrigued non-attendees with what exactly might have occurred, with a few carefully chosen words in the lodge records.

Lodge Amounderness 7105 (1951), period 1958-66 (excerpts)

The Lodge was opened in the Second Degree, regularly, and in the Third Degree, remarkably, by the Master.

Worshipful Brother Angus Gray delivered an address entitled briefly: "Some variations on Masonic Ritual emphasising the similarity of the essential basic principles to be found in the various rituals at present in use in the Masonic World, at the same time dissecting and commenting on differences of phraseology or linguistic expression encountered in the Rituals when dealing with specific situations in each of the three degrees." The Master and his Officers derived great comfort from the revelations resulting from the study.

The Lodge was opened by the Master in the Second Degree with aplomb and accuracy, and in the Third Degree with more aplomb and one of the Lodge variations.

On the presentation of the accounts, the Brethren appeared to be so struck by their magnificence that for some time they were unable to exclaim "O Wonderful Masons", but ultimately they were approved.

Brothers Holmes and Guyer having been made Fellowcrafts returned without aprons, eluded the Inner Guard, confounded the Deacons but not the Assistant Director of Ceremonies who, in a remarkable display of agility and exercising a twin pincer movement, simultaneously had them both correctly attired with utmost celerity.

Brother Guyer was conducted by the Master along the perilous lanes of the highway leading to the Third Degree. Skilfully evading the numerous obstacles thereon and bridging the valleys of amnesia with delicate structures original both in design and content, Master and pupil contrived to arrive simultaneously at the appointed destination with joy and exultation, and the Master resumed work in the First Degree most thankfully.

Canon John Adam was challenged by the Master, Canon Paul Schofield; the duel continued for several minutes, both Canons firing beautifully, and Brother Adam was raised in a manner conforming to the usages and customs of the English Constitution, subject to rearrangement by the Master.

The Master welcomed the Provincial Grand Master into the Lodge, surrendered the gavel and with charm, delicacy and dulcet tones suggested that its retention would afford him great relief. The Provincial Grand Master, gently chiding the Master for his departure from the usual formula, explained that relief could only be obtained after suffering, and he returned the gavel with great expectations.

Members of the Lodge

The Secretary deals with every member of the lodge, and should maintain an almost cradle-to-grave record for each one regarding his Masonic career and his continuing membership of the lodge. In an existing lodge there must already be a register of members with various personal and Masonic details entered therein, while new lodges obviously require a similar register to be started (BoC146). The personal details may include the addresses and telephone numbers for home and work, the names of the lady of the house and any children, perhaps the wedding anniversary, etc. The Masonic details should cover the dates of his initiation, passing, raising, occupying various offices up to the Chair and beyond, Provincial and Grand Lodge honours, etc. The former will be of use to other lodge Officers, such as the Treasurer, Almoner and Charity Steward, but all such information must be regarded as confidential within the confines of the lodge. Beware of the Data Protection Act: you must be careful how you store this information, especially if your lodge uses a website on the Internet for the benefit of members and visitors.

Starting a Masonic Career
As Secretary you should be contacted by his proposer and seconder and informed that they think a certain gentleman would be a useful member of the lodge and that they intend to put his name forward in the near future. This may occur as an informal contact or at a lodge or Lodge Committee meeting, and it may be only one person making the suggestion and looking for a seconder; the latter when found should have known the person for some time prior to the application going forward. The candidate will have to pay the necessary fees prior to his initiation (BoC169), the proposer and seconder being liable for his fees if he does not do so (BoC171). The gentleman (or proposer) should then write a formal letter to you as Secretary, expressing a wish to be considered as a candidate for Freemasonry and to become a member of your lodge in particular.

You will need to provide the proposer and seconder with an application form for them and their candidate to fill in certain personal details (BoC164). They should also be aware that there is a stipulation that the gentleman is over 21 years old except by dispensation (BoC157) and believes in a Supreme Being, otherwise his candidature cannot go further. The form is fairly self-explanatory, and when it is returned to you the interview by lodge members can be organised; if you have several candidates in the pipeline, you may choose to interview them individually but on the same night.

Your lodge bylaws may stipulate how many members constitute a quorum for the interview; if not, then consider having relatively few present rather than make the occasion too effacing by having dozens of people interviewing at a full Lodge Committee for example (BoC154). The Master if possible should chair the meeting and you as Secretary should be present. It would be preferable if the proposer and seconder could also attend, so the candidate has some recognisable faces around him, although if he has previously attended any social functions of the lodge, he perhaps already knows one or two other members. The interview should be conducted fairly informally, trying to put him at his ease and happy to talk about himself, and whether he has the support of his wife or partner. The members will not only be trying to ascertain whether or not he will make a good Mason, but also if he will fit in with the ambience of your lodge, and the more information he volunteers about himself then the clearer impression he will make. At the close of the interview he should be informed that his application will be put before the lodge and a ballot taken. If the ballot is successful, he will be informed on what night it is proposed that his Masonic career will commence, and hopefully he has already confirmed that he is able to attend regularly on lodge nights.

It is quite efficient to complete the remaining details on the form during or immediately after the interview rather than carrying or posting it round afterwards, and this is especially so if the candidate does not live or work within the catchment area of the lodge. There are many reasons why people do not choose to join local lodges, mainly centring on whom they know in Masonry, especially family, and whether or not they are able to attend on local lodge nights. For these candidates there is an extra hoop for their application to jump through; your Province has to write to the Province where they live or work and obtain clearance for them to join your lodge (BoC158, 161). You will need to explain why the candidate selected your lodge, possibly including a copy of the candidate's initial letter of interest if the reasons are set out there, and send the request for your Provincial Secretary to process the application further. The ballot for your candidate should not take place until confirmation has been received back from your Province that this course of action is acceptable, so this may create a slight time delay – often Provincial offices are very efficient in dealing with these confirmations, but you may not wish to set a very tight timescale between the interview and a possible initiation date, just in case.

If there are any problems with the candidate signing that he agrees with all of the queries on the form, or he has been recently prosecuted for any offence, the form will have to be referred to the Grand Secretary via Province. There is no need to declare convictions that are "spent" under the Rehabilitation of Offenders Act, and you can assure the candidate that offences such as parking and minor speeding fines will not bar anyone from joining Masonry, but the details need to be assessed by Grand Lodge before any further action can be taken. The Master can also tell the candidate that his proposer and seconder would not have put his name forward if they had any reservations, but sensibly the Craft is careful about who is allowed to come into the family.

The candidate will have to be formally proposed and seconded in open lodge at one meeting, and must be balloted for at the next regular meeting, otherwise he will have to be re-proposed (BoC159). Before the ballot takes place, you will have to read out the application form in lodge, or allude to the relevant details in the summons, as well as the statement of the Master in recommending the candidate as a suitable person to be made a Mason (BoC164). Similarly there is a 12-month time limit between a successful ballot and his initiation ceremony, otherwise there has to be a further re-proposal and ballot (BoC159). If the ballot goes against him, you will have to inform him of the outcome, and also advise his proposer and seconder that there needs to be a reasonable period before he should reapply for membership, and which may be specified in the lodge bylaws (BoC165). Some lodges, perhaps erring on the side of caution, circulate details about prospective candidates to their own lodge members and to nearby lodges, to allow any reservations to be voiced before the ballot is taken.

Assuming a successful ballot, you will need to write to him confirming the date for his initiation, and also advise him of the normal attire at a lodge meeting in England. His proposer and seconder can amplify for him any details you include in the letter as appropriate, and you might copy the letter to them. On his initiation night you will need him to sign the declaration book if he has not done so before and you will state in lodge that he has signed accordingly, just as the Treasurer may add that the requisite fee has been collected (this should come as no surprise to the candidate, as the interview or other discussions should have covered this aspect). You will need up-to-date copies of the Book of Constitutions and the lodge bylaws to be presented to him after the first part of the ceremony.

If the candidate comes from a family with other Masons, they may wish to attend his initiation, as may any of his friends who are on the Square. As long as he can provide you with the relevant names and addresses, you can send a summons to them in good time for them to be able to confirm their ability to attend or perhaps to send through you their good wishes after his first ceremony. If the candidate's father is a Mason, then his son will be a Lewis, and hopefully the father will be able to attend the meeting even if he is not a member of the lodge; if he is a member he will undoubtedly attend. It is a special occasion for both, and every courtesy should be extended, perhaps even inviting the father to participate in the ceremony – by delivering the charge, the North East corner, or the special father-son address at an initiation. There are occasions when a son has joined Freemasonry first and then the father joins; there is no similar son-father address, but again the son may be pleased to play a role in the family member's initiation, and the same obviously holds for family brothers before they become brothers again Masonically! In the case of a Lewis, note that he takes precedence over the other candidate(s) in a multiple initiation ceremony, but does not jump ahead of a queue of people on the waiting list to become members of the lodge.

Other candidates such as joining members (BoC163) and honorary members (BoC166-7) also have to fill in the same application form and there will have to be a ballot for their membership. In these cases there should be no need for an interview, especially if the joining member has already attended several times as a visitor and he is well known in your lodge. If he is from another Constitution, then he has to make a declaration on admission after the successful ballot or at least within one year (BoC163). Once a member of the English Constitution the joining member must wear English regalia in lodge, and it seems a little harsh that in doing so he should not wear a Past Master's collar until he has been through the chair of a lodge in the English Constitution, even if he has already done so in a lodge in his original Constitution.

After the candidate has been initiated or joined, you as Secretary and the Master sign the membership form and send it off to Grand Lodge via Province, together with the requisite registration fee. Some Provinces ask you to fill out two membership forms so that they can keep one and the lodge Secretary can send the other directly to the Grand Secretary with the fee. In these days of modern photocopiers, which can make back-to-back copies, the need for two forms seems somewhat outdated, and you will doubtless be keeping a photocopy for your lodge records.

For the joining and honorary members there are no ceremonies to go through, unless the joining member is not already a Master Mason, but the initiate obviously has the second and third degree ceremonies to complete. There must be at least a four-week gap between the separate degrees, except this can reduce by dispensation to one week in an overseas District (BoC90, 172). In your lodge bylaws, however, you may stipulate a longer period of time between the different degrees, rather than rush candidates through the degrees. Some candidates are unsure of the question and answer session at the start of their next degree, and in olden times in some lodges they would have been told that the ceremony had to be deferred until they could answer the questions competently. After his raising you again correspond with Grand Lodge or the District to inform it that there is a new Master Mason awaiting his Grand Lodge Certificate (BoC86-8, 174). This is usually sent back with efficient rapidity, although it may not be received in time for the following month's meeting, so it may be better to have received it before entering its presentation onto a future summons. You should note the date of his becoming a Master Mason, and the number of his Grand Lodge Certificate in the declaration book and also in the lodge members' records.

All of this for the candidate to take his first steps into the lodge and Grand Lodge records.

Progressing through the Offices of the Lodge

Fortunately the paperwork during the member's subsequent Masonic career is nowhere nearly as intense as his introduction to the Craft. If there is a progression of offices leading to the Master's chair, then he will enter it at the appropriate point and continue on upwards. The speed at which he starts his ascent to the Chair will be determined by his inclinations and capabilities, probably under the watchful eye of the Director of Ceremonies and other senior lodge members, and he may well have performed parts of the ceremonies before he is appointed to a lodge office. Many junior brethren are first asked to present the working tools of a degree to a candidate, and you as Secretary – in the role of recording the lodge business – will also be forming an opinion of how each junior is developing as a Mason and as a member of the lodge.

There is a caveat to mention to prospective Wardens; they must attend the installation meeting and be invested, or they are deemed not to have filled the office for an entire year (BoC109), and cannot be put forward to be Master Elect unless the Provincial Grand Master issues a dispensation. Often Province will write to warn a lodge as soon as it notices that the new Junior Warden was absent from the installation meeting, so that the Officer and the lodge are aware of the consequences of a further non-attendance at the next installation when he moves to Senior Warden.

Similarly the Master Elect has to attend his own installation as the new Master of the lodge. There is no mechanism whereby he can be made the Master of a lodge by proclamation if he has never been installed before, which can occur if a Master is continuing for a second year in office. With no installation able to take place, the outgoing Master also has no option but to stay in office (BoC107), as the ritual points out that he has to install his successor after being duly elected to be the head of the lodge. If there are any known complications about the Master Elect being able to attend on the standard installation day of the lodge, you had better start preparing to move the meeting, but check with Province about the latitude you have in the circumstances (BoC108). No-one can stay in the Master's chair for a third successive year, except by dispensation from the Provincial Grand Master, nor can anyone be a Master of two lodges at the same time, except by dispensation from the Grand Master (Metropolitan Areas and Provinces) or from the District Grand Master (BoC115).

Undertaking Offices as a Past Master

While progressing to the Master's chair, members will have filled most if not all of the offices from Tyler to Senior Warden, in other words seven of the nine regular Officers (BoC104), and possibly they have also been appointed to the additional offices of Steward and Assistant Secretary. The first job after being Master is Immediate Past Master, and then in some lodges – preferring to have an experienced member outside the door of the lodge – the IPM will next take on the office of Tyler.

That leaves the other two regular offices – Treasurer and Secretary – and the other six additional offices for a Past Master to fill in the future. There are usually few volunteers for Secretary or Treasurer, but even so most lodges prefer to see a succession of members filling these offices every few years, and indeed all of the regular offices must be individually filled by members (Tyler excepted) for the lodge to continue (BoC104). Obviously being a lodge Organist requires some musical skills, but this still leaves Chaplain, Director of Ceremonies and Assistant, Almoner and Charity Steward. Most lodges will want to fill all of these offices, as it shares out the workload, and it shows a collective willingness to support the lodge. The Secretary needs to keep a record of whatever offices each member takes on, so that a full history of his involvement in the lodge is maintained. If the member is a good ritualist, he will doubtless be asked to participate in future ceremonies. As Secretary you may additionally keep a record of when the member takes a prominent part in ceremonies, for example on Past Masters' Nights certain members may regularly volunteer to work particular sections of the different degrees, because they enjoy performing those parts of the ritual.

Provincial and Grand Lodge Honours

One of the pleasantest surprises for any Mason is to learn that he is to receive Provincial honours (BoC60-1, 66-70, see next chapter); indeed the subsequent promotions in Province and even appointment to Grand Officer status are also very pleasant, but by then the member knows a little more about the selection format. Each lodge is requested once a year to put forward members for first appointments or promotions by Province, although this may sometimes be directed through the Group system. The lodge may choose to limit such discussions to senior members of the lodge, so that the announcement will come as a surprise to the first-time recipient, but most Past Masters are aware of the normal time delay between leaving the Master's chair and the likelihood of receiving an honour. You as Secretary will be fully aware of what is going on, and you will doubtless have been a party to the decisions about the nominations. You should also note that while lodges can put forward recommendations for a member to receive Grand Lodge honours, with falling lodge memberships the appointments are becoming progressively more limited, and Grand Officers will become an even rarer species than they are currently.

The discussions will be based on what the brother has contributed to the lodge over the years, and there are many ways in which different brethren can apply their talents for the benefit of the lodge. Some may be excellent ritualists and regularly pressed into service; others may be good organisers – not only as Treasurer, Secretary and Director of Ceremonies, but also for lodge social occasions and other activities; others as organists may be in demand with other lodges. Also be aware that the Group organisation has a role to play in providing an independent assessment of the several lodge nominations, and do not be surprised by a request from Group for an idea of what a brother has contributed over the years, in and out of the lodge. This is where your record of that brother's Masonic career will be useful, and the electronic storage of lodge minutes will allow you rapidly to search on your computer through the various lodge meetings when he has played a significant role.

Although Past Masters can normally expect Provincial honours several years after their year as head of the lodge, there are also those stalwarts who contribute generously to the life of the lodge, but for personal or business reasons do not go through the Chair. Perhaps they just cannot cope with the ritual, or they find it difficult to attend every lodge meeting because they work on shifts or their jobs entail a significant amount of travel away from home, for example. However, they may be capable organisers of lodge social functions and other activities, or are able to use their artistic abilities in creating table plans for Ladies' Evenings or menus for Olde English Nights, etc. When their contributions are recognised by Province, to some extent it can engender more pleasure among the lodge members than those honours that have been almost semi-automatically gained by Past Masters, and undoubtedly you as Secretary will have played an important role in ensuring that the full extent of each brother's contribution has been set down for others to assess. In Provinces there is no distinction between Past Masters and others in receiving Past Provincial Grand Rank, but in London Past Masters attain Metropolitan Grand

Rank, and those who have never been through the Chair receive Metropolitan Rank (BoC61, 68).

You will obviously have to update your members' records when they receive Provincial or Grand Lodge appointments and promotions, and do not forget the various corrections that will be required on the future summonses and other lodge literature, but this particular chore brings an enjoyable perspective to your duties.

Departure from Membership

While noting each member's participation in the lodge as a cradle-to-grave record, you will have to stop any further entries when he is no longer a member. This may be for pleasant reasons, such as being made an honorary member, gaining promotion at work perhaps in an organisation with several sites and the vacancy being elsewhere in the country, or by changing jobs and job location. It may be for less pleasant reasons, such as non-payment of lodge subscriptions or for disciplinary reasons, or even for sad reasons such as being called to the Grand Lodge Above.

The lodge can make a member of any regular lodge an honorary member of the lodge, and frequently this is done to thank a senior brother for many years of service in the lodge. However, the member concerned should be aware that, apart from not having to pay any subscription (and the lodge not being charged by Province or Grand Lodge for his honorary membership), his right to vote in propositions put to the lodge is forfeit, and he only retains the right to propose new members into the lodge (BoC166-7). Sometimes lodges have been surprised, when discussing the honorary status with the intended recipient, that it is vigorously refused – it is not always easy to silence old dogs in this way! Another reason for a refusal may be that, while an honorary member is allowed to visit his own lodge as often as he wants, he cannot visit any other lodge more than once unless he is still a subscribing member of at least one lodge, just as with an unattached brother who has resigned in good standing with his lodge (BoC127). Surprisingly some Provinces stipulate that only subscribing brethren will receive a 50/60/70/80-year certificate from the Provincial office, for which an honorary member will automatically be excluded, which seems harsh when the honorary membership was offered in gratitude for services rendered, but fortunately others are not so pernickety. Occasionally lodges will confer honorary membership on a Mason who is not a lodge member, perhaps for assisting in arranging regular reciprocal visits or other joint and enjoyable activities between lodges often some distance apart, and possibly from other Constitutions, and this honour is almost always accepted with gratitude.

A member can resign from his lodge by writing to the Secretary or orally in open lodge (BoC183), or from the Craft by writing to the Grand Secretary (BoC183A).

For the member who has to resign for family or business reasons, you are required to furnish him with a clearance certificate stating that he has left the lodge in good standing, as he will need this if he is looking to join a lodge in his new locality (BoC175). In fact you can be of further assistance here, because you can find out some useful telephone contact numbers from the Secretary of the Province with jurisdiction over where the brother is moving to. These can include details of lodge or Group Secretaries in the vicinity of his new home, and if he holds off resigning from your lodge until he has found a new lodge then he can visit a few local lodges, and perhaps take his lady along to one or two social events, so that both can gain a feel for the lodges and choose one with which they are both comfortable. Some members apply to their mother lodge for a country or non-dining membership, which will have to be formally agreed by the lodge, and means they pay a reduced fee.

Possibly more of this introductory service could be provided by lodges or Groups, because moving regions within England and Wales is one of the most common ways in which Masons are lost from Masonry. We are all part of one universal Masonic family, so why not assist a member to settle down quickly in his new location, with local Masons calling in to make sure everything is being coped with? And assuming that he joins a new lodge, he will probably reappear in yours for special occasions, and it would be nice to keep in touch with him even if it is not your immediate responsibility to do so, while it is equally up to him to retain contact with the lodge he has left.

You should also be aware that every current member of the lodge at some time may require a clearance certificate of good standing, especially if he wants to visit lodges in London or abroad such as in the USA. He can prove himself and he will have his Grand Lodge Certificate, but certain areas of this country and the world are keen to see that his lodge membership has not lapsed, and a receipt from the Treasurer may suffice in proving this or you as Secretary may write a short letter to this effect on the lodge's headed notepaper.

If a member seems to lose touch with the lodge, perhaps because of pressure of work, a lengthy illness or other family problems, then you as Secretary or the Almoner should check if the lodge can do anything to help. You will after all be checking the attendance sheet after every lodge meeting, so you are likely to be the first to know that someone is increasingly absent. If the absences continue, and he is late or misses paying his subscription, then he is heading for exclusion, and it may be that a timely call or visit can gently persuade him to redevelop the habit of attending lodge meetings – there is the old saying: "A stitch in time…" And if you feel someone else in the lodge knows him better than you do personally, then ask this member to make contact and check that he is fit and well, and why he is not attending lodge.

The less happy partings are those involving the avoidance of paying subscriptions or disciplinary matters (BoC179-82). The lodge bylaws will state what time period there is between the subscriptions being due and action taken over non-payment, and the Treasurer should warn a member in arrears that time is running out. In any case, Grand Lodge decrees that, in the absence of any other time period being stated, after two years of paying no dues, he ceases to be a member of the lodge – this is automatic, and no vote is required (BoC148). The lodge may ask you as Secretary to inform the member that he is approaching the time for automatic exclusion, probably by a telephone call if you cannot visit him. If there is no positive response forthcoming, you then should send him a letter by Recorded Delivery with advice of delivery and marked "Private and Confidential" not less than 14 days before the matter is to be discussed formally by the lodge.

He may choose to attend the meeting or not; a ballot will be taken at that meeting, and if two-thirds of those present vote in favour he will be excluded. You should then write to inform him of the outcome, and also inform the Provincial and Grand Secretaries (BoC181). He is still entitled to a clearance certificate, but on this occasion the reason for the exclusion must be included, as he may eventually wish to join another lodge, and that lodge is liable for his outstanding arrears, so it will need to be aware of this before accepting him into membership (BoC163). If and when he is able and wishes to pay off his arrears, you again inform both of the above Secretaries, but the brother, if he wishes to rejoin the lodge, will have to be formally proposed and balloted for again (BoC181). Although non-payment of subscriptions is the most common cause for exclusion, any disciplinary matters are dealt with in exactly the same way.

One day even those that do not resign eventually have to leave membership of the lodge, when they die. You as Secretary should be among the first to know, and you will have to promptly contact all the other lodge members to inform them, possibly waiting only until the funeral arrangements have been made so that you can pass on those details. The Almoner should liaise directly with the family to see if the lodge can be of any assistance, but if previously the deceased and his family had enjoyed good health, the lodge Secretary is the most likely member for the widow to have talked to a number of times, and she may turn to you as a friendly voice if not face. If the deceased was a senior Provincial or even Grand Officer, then you should also inform not only the Group Secretary but also the Provincial Secretary, who can advise you if someone from Province will be at the funeral. The same notifications apply if the member were a lodge Officer, and the Master may be required to appoint a replacement as soon as possible, which needs to be itemised on the agenda of the next lodge meeting. You may also decide as a lodge that the next summons should bear the record that the member has died, and one of his closer friends may be invited to give a short epitaph of his life and Masonic career at the start of the next lodge meeting. In this case the friend may wish to check some brief details of the deceased's time in the lodge, and your individual members' records will come in useful again.

If the Master or Treasurer should die, or become too incapacitated to continue in office, then the Provincial office and the Group Secretary need to be informed as soon as possible. If the Master dies he cannot be replaced, and the Senior Warden will have to summon the lodge to future meetings, although the IPM or another installed Master will occupy the Master's chair (BoC119). The Treasurer, being an elected office, will require a dispensation from Province to hold an interim election (BoC112). The untimely death or incapacity of a Master Elect between his election and installation will require actions to be taken, depending on the time this occurs before the installation meeting, as discussed before (BoC106-7).

Aspects of the Rules (concerning Members)

BoC76 – only the Grand Master can sanction the erasure of a lodge or the expulsion of a brother.

BoC86-88 – District Grand Masters can issue Grand Lodge Certificates directly, instead of via the Grand Secretary, as is the case for all Metropolitan Areas and Provinces.

BoC90 – in lodges abroad, and by dispensation of the District Grand Master or the Grand Secretary as appropriate, a brother may be advanced to a higher degree in less than four weeks (BoC172), but not in less than one week.

BoC127 – if a brother resigns from membership of his only lodge in good standing, he becomes unattached, and as such can visit any other lodge only once until he again becomes a subscribing member of a lodge, and this restriction also applies to honorary members who can only attend their own lodge as often as they wish but not others, unless they remain a subscribing member of another lodge.

BoC146 – every lodge shall keep a register of its members, present and past.

BoC148 – a brother ceases to be a member of a lodge if his subscription remains unpaid for two years, or shorter time if stated in the lodge bylaws; and the Secretary shall inform the Grand Secretary when and if that brother pays off his arrears.

BoC157 – no person shall be made a Mason under 21 years of age, except by dispensation of the Provincial Grand Master.

BoC158 – if a person wants to be made a Mason in a lodge that is not near to where he lives or works, he must state his reasons and his application must be referred by the lodge's Provincial Secretary to his counterpart with jurisdiction over the applicant's domestic or business residence.

BoC159 – a candidate shall be proposed and seconded at a regular meeting of the lodge, balloted for at the next regular meeting and, if successful, initiated within one year of the ballot or his election shall be void; the printed application forms are supplied by the Grand Secretary (*Province may hold a stock of them*).

BoC161 – no lodge shall initiate a person residing in an area under the jurisdiction of the Grand Lodges of Ireland or Scotland without the agreement of the respective Grand Secretary (*via its own Provincial Grand Secretary*), excepting persons in the Armed Services or at a university with a lodge specially attached to that university.

BoC162 – every candidate for initiation must previously sign a witnessed declaration.

BoC163 – a joining or rejoining member is proposed and seconded at one meeting, balloted for at the next (or the proposal is void), and must take up membership within one year of the ballot (or the ballot is void); he must produce his Grand Lodge Certificate (or a substitute from the Grand Secretary if his lodge has ceased to exist) and his lodge clearance certificate(s); and if the brother was excluded for non-payment of dues, the new lodge shall be liable for all arrears; and a brother from another Constitution has to make a declaration to obey all the rules of Grand Lodge on election or within one year of it.

BoC164 – a candidate shall fill in the application form honestly; if he cannot complete any part without qualification, the application will be referred to the Grand Secretary for certification to proceed with the ballot; once admitted the application form must be signed by the lodge Secretary and together with the registration fee be sent to the Grand Secretary, with normally a copy of the form being sent to the Provincial Grand Secretary; the candidate's particulars and the Master's certificate shall be read out prior to the ballot for membership.

BoC166 – a lodge has the power to elect any member as an honorary member, and the lodge will not be liable for Grand Lodge or Provincial Grand Lodge dues on his behalf.

BoC167 – a lodge can make a member of a regular lodge an honorary member, for whom no fees are paid to or by the lodge, and who cannot vote or make any proposition in the lodge except – if he is a Past Master of the lodge – that of proposing candidates for lodge membership.

BoC169 – a candidate for Masonry shall pay the full initiation fees on or before his initiation.

BoC171 – the proposer and seconder of any candidate for lodge membership are liable for all lodge fees applicable.

BoC172 – a lodge cannot confer a higher degree on a member within an interval less than four weeks after the previous degree was conferred; the Grand Master may grant a dispensation retrospectively validating the ceremony if he deems it appropriate.

BoC174 – applications for a member's Grand Lodge Certificate must be sent by the member's lodge and, although normally issued to Master Masons, can also be specially issued after the first and second degrees and later exchanged free of charge for a certificate for a higher degree; the certificate should where possible be presented in open lodge and immediately signed by the recipient, or sent by registered post if circumstances dictate that; replacement certificates can be supplied for a fee.

BoC175 – a certificate shall be provided free of charge by the lodge to confirm the member is in good standing with the lodge, or has left the lodge in good standing or other stated circumstances, including exclusion or suspension.

BoC176 – any connection by a member with quasi-Masonic organisations, before or during membership of the lodge, must be referred to the Provincial Grand Master.

BoC179 – if a lodge suspends a member, or the lodge itself is suspended, the member is still liable to pay all dues.

BoC179A – any member who receives a custodial or suspended sentence must report it to the Master of his lodge or directly to the Grand Secretary if unattached.

BoC180 – any brother disturbing the harmony of the lodge may be censured or excluded for the remainder of the meeting.

BoC181 – by resolution in a meeting, a lodge may exclude any member permanently from the lodge, provided at least two-thirds of those present vote in favour; notification of the exclusion and the causes thereof shall be sent to the Grand Secretary and the Provincial Grand Secretary; and if the exclusion was for non-payment of dues, both Secretaries shall be informed when the Brother pays off his arrears.

BoC182 – the Provincial Grand Master may order the member's reinstatement upon appeal, or suspend the lodge if it refuses to do so.

BoC183 – any member may resign from his lodge orally in open lodge or in writing to the lodge Secretary.

BoC183A – a brother may resign from the Craft in writing on the appropriate form, and by sending it to the Grand Secretary, and the brother must surrender his Grand Lodge Certificate, which will be returned to him by the Grand Secretary when he is to be proposed and seconded as a joining or rejoining member of a lodge.

External Liaisons

Grand Lodge

One of your duties is to ensure that the Grand Lodge returns are sent at the required time to the Grand Secretary. There are two returns, the annual return which is due within one month of the end of the subscription year (BoC146), and an installation return which is required to be sent after the installation meeting (BoC151). If your installation occurs at the end of the financial year you will be somewhat busy, as parts or all of the forms have to be filled in manually; we have not yet moved totally to the electronic age. The annual return is, however, usefully already supplied on a computer print-out by Grand Lodge and is sent for you to update it. So one of the first items when you receive the return is to check that last year's changes have been fully noted. Grand Lodge dues are calculated a full year in arrears, so you add any initiates or members who have joined during the previous 12 months and which have not yet been included by Grand Lodge. Unless you have a very legible handwriting style, you would probably be better completing the form in capital letters for clarity – many lodge Secretaries have their returns sent back because their writing is illegible, and Grand Lodge wants to record the information accurately.

You also annotate where brethren have resigned, died, ceased membership or been excluded, and also those who have been made honorary members during the past year. The lodge still has to pay a year's dues for each such member, even for a part-year membership, but the return that is sent by Grand Lodge for the following year will have eliminated those who have left the lodge. As Grand Lodge relies on your input when calculating next year's dues, you should only have yourself to blame if next time you are being charged too much because you omitted to inform them that somebody had left the lodge (BoC148). You then need a cheque from the Treasurer for the required total amount of money which is normally the amount requested by Grand Lodge – you will receive a credit in the following year if any of their records were out of date – before you mail it off. The form is in triplicate, so the top copy goes to Grand Lodge with the cheque, the second to Province, and the third is for you to keep; and ensure the three forms are perfectly aligned when filling them in, otherwise some data may be going into the wrong columns and will cause confusion.

You will also note that each member is given a unique Grand Lodge number, which will stay with him throughout his Masonic career, and is noted on his Grand Lodge Certificate. This enables the Grand Secretary to calculate the number of Masons in the English Constitution, noting that several Masons belong to more than one lodge. For example, many join an Installed Masters' lodge once they have attained the chairs of their own lodges, and merely summating the individual lodge memberships can significantly overestimate how many Masons there really are.

The installation return still requires you manually to fill in the required data, and is the one which identifies the Principal Officers and all Past Masters – both of the lodge and those who have been through the Chairs of other lodges. All of these brethren are eligible to attend Grand Lodge, as long as they remain subscribing members of yours or another lodge (BoC9, 151), and its meetings are held on the second Wednesdays of March, June, September and December. When they present themselves at the entrance of the Grand Lodge meeting room, they will be checked by scrutineers that they are on the installation returns and therefore entitled to be present, so your return becomes their passport into the meeting, and attendees should wear their formal collars of office. If a Warden was absent at the installation meeting, you leave the date of his investiture blank and still send the return promptly, but you have to write to Province and Grand Lodge to advise them at which lodge meeting he was afterwards invested. You should note that, if a member has been appointed and served as a Warden in a lodge, but has not continued through to the Master's chair, he cannot attend Grand Lodge; only acting Wardens and Installed/Past Masters can do so.

You will have therefore to add all Past Masters who have joined your lodge in the past year, and also the Immediate Past Master if he had not been a Master before his term of office last year. You should also place the Past Masters in chronological order of them individually becoming a Master, placing a Past Master of the lodge above a Past Master in the lodge but in the same year. The other additional information required includes the names and addresses of the Master, Secretary, Almoner and Charity Steward, of which at least the first is likely to change each year, and then you and the Master sign the document before sending it to the Grand Secretary. And do not underestimate the severity with which late returns will be viewed (BoC152), so it would be better if you are not tempted to put off the evil day any longer than you have to. Although one reason for the separate form is that the lodge installation may be several months away from the end of the lodge financial year, and both returns are expected within a month of the installation/year end, it is a pity that one suitably modified form, preferably computerised, cannot perform both functions.

The other main dealings with the Grand Secretary, such as candidates' application forms, requests for Grand Lodge Certificates, and brethren who have ceased to be members by resignation or otherwise, have been dealt with previously. Changes to the lodge name or its permanent meeting place, etc., will be covered in the next chapter.

Your lodge may be fortunate that one of your members may be considered for appointment to Grand Rank, though as stated before these opportunities will become rarer as the number of honours each year is shrinking with the decreasing memberships and numbers of lodges. It is the Provincial Grand Master who personally recommends such appointments, but you can be sure he will have discussed the possibilities with his Deputy and Assistants, and also with the Group Chairmen. For those who attain Grand Rank, they and a few guests are invited to London on the last Wednesday in April to be invested, and Supreme Grand Chapter holds its equivalent meeting on the Thursday following.

Provincial Grand Lodge
Province also requires its own return from each lodge (BoC149), as well as possibly requesting a copy of each Grand Lodge return. The Provincial return may be based on a calendar year rather than the lodges' financial years, and may have its own Provincial number for each Mason rather than using his unique Grand Lodge number, which can be confusing, but some returns are computerised like the Grand Lodge version. Some Provinces even want their own installation return, which is odd as the Grand Lodge return has all of the up-to-date information. And Province is also more demanding than Grand Lodge, in that Provincial dues are required of every new member in his year of entry, instead of waiting until the following full year of membership.

All of this seems a largely unnecessary quadruplication of information and, although the layouts of the forms are becoming similar, we have not yet managed to create one form containing all of the data necessary to both organisations, but could this be a future aim of Grand and Provincial Grand Lodges? After all, a single column on the annual return could indicate who are Past or Installed Masters and therefore entitled to attend Grand Lodge, by stating the date of each member's first installation, and perhaps in the remarks column "WM", "SW", "JW" and "IPM" could indicate who are these Officers and the latest Past Master. And if the Secretary, Almoner and Charity Steward all continue in office, why have to write out their contact details over and over again? To keep copying out the list of Past Masters onto two forms on a yearly basis must be incredibly tiring for the

Secretaries of lodges of Installed Masters and others with memberships exceeding 100 – can we not do better in this 21st Century? An image of Bob Cratchitt suggests itself, bending over a desk dimly lit by candlelight, copying reams of names onto endless forms while Scrooge looks on, but surely this was a story from the 19th Century? If placing Past Masters in date order is truly important to Province or Grand Lodge, then let them use an installation date column to order them electronically in their records, and they can also check all Masons from their individual numbers in any case. Probably from the viewpoint of the lodge it is the date they joined or went through the Chair of the lodge that is the critical issue, and this order does not need rewriting for every newly joined Past Master. With a little sensible design it should be possible to create a single form that meets all the requirements of Province and Grand Lodge, and perhaps one day find a secure method of electronically transferring the data. The advent of two computerised print-out returns is already a very useful step forward, but with a little more effort...

The timescale for sending the lodge return to Province will be detailed in the Provincial bylaws, and again prompt returns and payments of fees makes life in the Provincial office very much easier. And being purely selfish, you will want to be on good terms with the staff in the Provincial office. There will be many occasions when a quick telephone call to them will elicit all the information you need to cover an unusual occurrence in your lodge, for example your lodge may suffer the death of a Master for the first time in its history. Even if some of your lodge's ideas for other activities are still in the planning stage, Province can point out the best and most efficient course of action to follow in order to achieve a satisfactory outcome in whatever you are thinking of doing. In their position, at the hub of all activities in the Province, they will have come across almost every eventuality covered by the Book of Constitutions, and local bylaws and traditions, and they are always willing to help those who seek their advice.

Province will also require several routine items from you such as copies of your lodge summonses, a number to be sent to the Provincial office or individually and directly to the senior Provincial Officers. They want copies of new membership forms that you are sending to Grand Lodge, and possibly also the letter requesting a Grand Lodge Certificate for a new Master Mason. Many Provinces will send to new lodge Secretaries information sheets detailing the various tasks they request the Officer to assist them with, and very useful guides these can be, while others are putting such advice onto their websites. Province will also liaise with you regarding who is to represent the Provincial Grand Master at your next installation and who will be accompanying him, which is useful for planning your catering arrangements. As Secretary, you should write to welcome the representative to the lodge, including with the letter a summons and perhaps a map of how to find the

Hall. You might also ask him if he would like to participate in the ceremony in any way; in some Groups it is traditional to ask the representative to give the address to the brethren or a similar role, and it is courteous to enquire what he would like to do during his visit. You might also ask if he has any special dietary requirements, which hopefully can be catered for, and what time he expects to arrive so that someone can be at the Hall to meet him.

Province will also nominate someone senior to attend the lodge on major personal and lodge landmarks, such as 50+ years in Masonry for members and centenary or higher lodge celebrations. They will also notify you if they are holding workshops for lodge Directors of Ceremonies, or meetings regarding the Provincial Festivals, and for the latter the lodges will probably be visited by a member of the Festival committee to encourage further contributions towards the funds already collected. Province will need to be aware of any deaths in the lodge, and especially the Master or Treasurer as elected Officers, and of any exclusions and the reasons for them. Province will advise you when a senior Provincial or Grand Officer has died, and over what period of time it is required that lodge Officers wear black rosettes as a sign of mourning and the lodge summons is to be printed in black or edged in black as a mark of respect.

You will also have to apply to Province for a dispensation if you want to move the lodge meeting day or place. Both might be required for a special lodge event, perhaps moving to the consecration date for a major lodge anniversary, and the former if your regular lodge meeting clashes with a prohibited day or a Bank Holiday for example and you wish to move the meeting by more than seven days (BoC139). If the lodge has temporary problems with the premises in which it meets, you may require a temporary dispensation for the length of time that the lodge will have to meet elsewhere. If the lodge wants a permanent move, then the Province and the Group(s) involved will need to sanction the transfer, and if the new premises are in a different Province, then the new Province will also have to liaise over the move (BoC142). If the lodge requires to hold an emergency meeting, another dispensation will have to be sought (BoC140), while Province is also able to advise on the wearing of Masonic jewels, etc., outside purely Masonic meetings (BoC178).

It has already been said that receiving the first Provincial honours should always be a pleasure. There is little doubt that under normal circumstances the greater the contribution of the individual, the higher the initial Provincial honour will be. On the other hand there is no point in any member of your lodge being disappointed by the first Provincial rank he has received; Groups and Provinces have to balance the merits of brethren throughout their jurisdictions, and some years there may be a plethora of very deserving Masons to be considered, and Provinces are strictly limited in the number of appointments they can confer in any one year (BoC68). As Secretary and with a knowledge of how the system works, you can perhaps prevent any discord over honours which are somehow disappointing, noting that it may not be too long before a further promotion rectifies an apparent anomaly, because often after a period of time a past Provincial Officer may receive a promotion in rank. Although the number of these promotions within a Province are not currently limited, as are the first appointments, again with falling lodge memberships limits could be imposed in future and such promotions become rarer.

Local Group

In the larger Provinces there are usually local groupings of lodges, and there will be a Group Chairman appointed by the Provincial Grand Master to oversee local matters. He will probably have a Group Secretary, and you will be liaising with him on a regular basis. The Group Chairman or one of his committee may be required to attend the lodge installations, as a courtesy to the representative of the Provincial Grand Master, and the lodge Secretary will be informed in good time who is to attend. If your lodge is running into any kind of difficulty, perhaps through a decreasing membership, then the Group Officers will be able to furnish advice in addition to Province as above, and possibly also provide some support while the lodge decides on its future.

There will also be Group meetings, and your lodge will be required to elect a formal representative so that he can be briefed on all aspects of Group activities, as well as raising any matters that your lodge may wish to air at such meetings. He could be the person who puts forward the members whom the lodge considers as meriting their first or subsequent Provincial honours, and he may therefore liaise with you for the details of what different members have done throughout their careers in the lodge. The Group might organise meals where all of the local Masters can meet each other and perhaps agree to avoid clashing with each other's socials and Ladies' Evenings, and also organise meals for recent Entered Apprentices, Fellowcrafts and Master Masons and perhaps their ladies to meet the Group Officers and their ladies as an informal welcome to Masonry in the area. The Group may also request that each lodge sends a copy of its summons to each of the other lodges in the Group to promote inter-visiting.

Masonic Hall

The organisation of practice meetings and lodge committee meetings has already been discussed from the viewpoint of the lodge, but your arrangements will have to fit in with the other lodges and side degrees that share the facilities. In large Masonic Halls, such as those to be found in the centres of the larger cities, the number of lodges is well into double if not treble figures, and the lodge possessions may be stored in lockable cupboards or wheelable containers. With the latter it is probable that the Hall will arrange delivery and collection of the equipment before and after any of your meetings in the lodge rooms, but your members will probably have to arrive early in order to set out the lodge room, just as you would have to do if you have your own static storage facilities. If there is any additional equipment that you require, perhaps owned by the Hall for the benefit of all lodges, you as Secretary will have to order it before the meeting to ensure its delivery to your lodge room, and there is even more need to check on arrival that everything is as you expected; and if you rent non-Masonic premises for your meetings, similar storage arrangements will apply.

All buildings require maintenance from time to time, whether for redecoration or other purposes. Sadly this costs money and the only way of raising it is from the lodges and side degrees which meet there. In fact the burden usually falls on the lodges, as many lodge members are in the side degrees meeting in the same building, and the money may be raised on a lodge basis or by a *per capita* charge. The Hall committee may also decide to organise some fundraising events for all of the lodges to enjoy, as a way of spreading the pain more equally. During redecoration phases, if these cannot be done during the summer or winter recesses, it may mean some shuffling of meeting and practice rooms while the work is going on, and all of the occupants will hopefully be able to work harmoniously around the problem.

As well as holding the lodge meeting, many lodges arrange the festive board on the same premises, while some choose to dine elsewhere. In the larger Masonic Halls there are not only several lodge rooms, but several dining rooms. Just as you will try to book a larger meeting room for your installation meeting and any other special meetings where you expect a bumper attendance, you will also try to book a larger dining room to accommodate the increased numbers. Some of the Halls will also have outside lets for their dining facilities, so there may be clashes with external organisations as well as between different Masonic bodies. To cover all of the possible permutations, you would be well advised to be early in confirming your lodge bookings and anticipated numbers, so that you are provided with suitable dining facilities and run less risk of being seriously overcrowded at the meeting or meal.

The caterers may well introduce some organisational rules of their own, even those which include the members' ladies assisting with the provision of the food. They do not want to go to the time and expense of preparing 70 meals to find that only 35 people turn up, and many caterers will expect recompense for all excess meals. Over the years your lodge will have a reasonable idea of how many people attend the different meetings, and many caterers ask lodges to estimate within say ±10% what the numbers will be, perhaps a week or less in advance. With microwave ovens and frozen foods it should not be difficult for them to prepare some additional meals if the numbers at a meeting exceed expectations, but more than 10% in the reverse direction will almost always incur penalties. With this in mind, some lodges have introduced a pre-paid meal booking system, insisting on cash with order, and then rely on the caterers finding the extra meals as and when required. If your lodge operates such a system, you will be sending out booking slips with the summons, and these may need to be produced for each meal if the prices vary. Armed with the replies, either you or the Treasurer will inform the caterers of the number of meals required by the appointed day, which the Tyler will confirm on the night – especially for the extras. And if your members or any regular visitors have special dietary needs, the caterers should be pre-warned how many vegetarian meals, for example, are required.

Aspects of the Rules (concerning External Liaisons)

BoC9 – every installed Master can attend Grand Lodge as long as he is a subscribing member of a lodge in the English Constitution.

BoC60 – the Grand Master has the power to form London or any other specified area in England and Wales into a Metropolitan Area; and a Metropolitan Grand Master may appoint a Deputy Metropolitan Grand Master and a number of Metropolitan Group Chairmen.

BoC61 – a Metropolitan Grand Master can appoint annually Past Masters to Metropolitan Grand Rank and can appoint Master Masons to Metropolitan Rank according to the size of the Metropolitan Area; and he can at his discretion promote brethren holding Metropolitan Grand Rank to Senior Metropolitan Grand Rank.

BoC66 – a Provincial Grand Master may appoint a Deputy Provincial Grand Master and a number of Assistant Provincial Grand Masters according to the size of the Province.

BoC68 – a Provincial Grand Master can appoint annually acting Officers and Past Provincial ranks according to the size of his Province; and the Grand Master may authorise additional celebratory Past Ranks.

BoC69 – a Provincial Grand Master may appoint additional past ranks to brethren holding past ranks in other Provinces when they have joined his Province.

BoC70 – a Provincial Grand Master may promote Provincial Grand Officers at his discretion.

BoC73 – only Past Masters can be promoted to Past Provincial Grand Warden.

BoC122 – the Grand Master, Pro Grand Master, Deputy Grand Master and Assistant Grand Master can preside over any lodge; the Provincial Grand Master, Pro Provincial Grand Master, Deputy Provincial Grand Master and Assistant

Provincial Grand Masters can preside over any lodge in their Province; and the Metropolitan Grand Master, Pro Metropolitan Grand Master and Deputy Metropolitan Grand Master can preside over any lodge in the Metropolitan Area, and the Metropolitan Group Chairmen can preside over any lodge in their own Metropolitan Group.

BoC146-7 – every lodge Secretary shall send in the Grand Lodge annual return within one month of the end of the lodge subscription year, together with the requisite fees.

BoC149 – every lodge Secretary shall send in the Provincial Grand Lodge annual return similarly to that to Grand Lodge, together with the requisite fees.

BoC150 – brethren excluded by lodges for non-payment of dues may appeal against the exclusion.

BoC151 – every lodge Secretary shall send to the Grand Secretary a return of all members eligible to attend Grand Lodge (Wardens, Master and Past Masters of and in the lodge), with addresses of the Master, Secretary, Almoner and Charity Steward, and the Master and Secretary shall sign the return.

BoC152 – any lodge neglecting to make its returns and payments for a period of six months shall be liable to erasure or a lesser penalty.

BoC178 – brethren shall not wear Masonic jewels or badges outside purely Masonic meetings except by dispensation from the Provincial Grand Master.

Other Routine and Non-Routine Matters

Lodge Bylaws

Each lodge has to draft its own rules of administration (BoC136-8, 154). With an established lodge, these will have been well developed over the years, which may need alteration from time to time, and if you are forming a new lodge you will have to draft new bylaws. Grand Lodge has a model set of bylaws which should form the basis of your own particular requirements, and even if you are only altering your existing bylaws, you may be well advised to obtain a copy from the Grand Secretary – to see if some simple revisions could significantly reduce the need for further regular alterations. For example, changing the bylaws with each change of subscription can easily be avoided with a slight rewording of the text. There is no need to go to the extreme of one 19th Century West Lancashire lodge, whose first bylaws ran to over 10,000 words, but the author McGlinchy was of Irish descent!

Every time you make any changes to the bylaws, you have to give notice in lodge that you are proposing to do so, and in the next lodge summons you have to detail the exact wording that you will be substituting, so that each member knows what is being proposed, even if he did not attend the previous meeting. All discussion on this topic should have been exhausted in the Lodge Committee, but the lodge may tolerate some further limited discussion in open lodge if necessary, before putting it to the vote by a show of hands. If the changes are accepted, you then have to create three copies of the new bylaws and a statement at which lodge meeting they were adopted, signed by you and the Master, and send all three to the Provincial Secretary for him to send to the Grand Secretary for ratification. Grand Lodge retains one copy, Province keeps one of the two returned, and sends the third to the lodge duly authorised. This process can take some time, so experienced Treasurers, who cannot exact any increase in subscription before their bylaws have been authorised, will propose any change well before they hope to implement it.

Secretarial Paraphernalia

Many lodges present their Secretaries on their investiture with a briefcase, and you will rapidly learn why! You will soon find out that you will be expected to carry all sorts of items with you to any meeting, so if you think that you merely will be carrying the Minute Books of the lodge and Lodge Committee, the Tyler's book/sheet, a spare pen and paper, and a few extra summonses, think again. Those items you will certainly need, and also the relevant sections of your correspondence file because some members may want the details of any item that you report on during the risings, and it will be more efficient to answer their queries instantly rather than by telephone or letter at a later date.

You would be advised to carry an up-to-date copy of the Book of Constitutions, in case anything arises in the lodge meeting that necessitates reference to it. You may also adopt the habit of carrying a second copy, so that you are always prepared for the presentation of a copy to an initiate at his first ceremony or the Master at his installation (BoC138). For the same reason you will have a few copies of your lodge bylaws, for the Master when installed, for new members, and for any existing members who may request a further copy. Some lodges additionally present the initiate with a copy of the charge that was delivered to him during the ceremony, as one of the few pieces of ritual which can be shown to family members and friends, and hopefully allay any residual reservations they may harbour about his becoming a Mason. Lodges sometimes provide candidates with the appropriate Peterborough booklets on the individual ceremonies when they proceed through them.

You will doubtless carry a copy of your lodge ritual with you. Some lodges will present a new Master Mason with his own copy of the ritual, and if the Emulation version is close to the one used in your lodge, then that book may suffice for him to begin his learning. Again there is the possibility that another lodge member will ask for a copy of the ritual, and you will be seen at your helpful and efficient best if you are able to immediately accommodate the request.

For certain lodge meetings there will be several propositions and ballots, and you may be expected to write out those propositions (for lodge representatives on various bodies for example) so that you can delegate various members to read them out in lodge. This usefully saves you from proposing almost everything and the Treasurer seconding everything, although some lodges seem quite happy with this system as the norm. For the business meetings to elect the Master and Treasurer, and the Tyler if required, you will have to provide voting slips for the members to use in the ballots.

Another item that is sometimes requested is a map of where the lodge meets, if for example a member is inviting a guest to the next meeting and wants to advise him how to find the building. He may of course request you to post a copy of the next summons to the guest, and you can then include a map at the same time. And you may also have prepared a table plan for the brethren to check where they are to be seated at the festive board, and possibly place cards as well. All in all, the briefcase should be filling up quite nicely.

Inventory of the Lodge Furniture

One of the pieces of information that you will inherit on becoming lodge Secretary is the inventory of the lodge regalia. This will normally be checked every year and any new items will be added to an amended list and any missing items noted and searched for among the members. The artefacts may be stored in a locked lodge cupboard or box which will usually have a limited number of keys, often for the Master, Secretary, Director of Ceremonies and Tyler. Many lodges have items of considerable value, particularly those lodges dating from the 18th Century when the Officers' jewels would be made of a variety of precious metals, which is why they are stored under lock and key for security and insurance reasons. It should be noted that the Master and Wardens temporarily own in trust all of the lodge possessions that are not already vested in special trustees (BoC143).

In these days with computerised records, it is an easy matter to update the inventory listing as required and, as you will probably be involved in the annual stocktake, you might also note the condition of the different items of regalia. Officers' collars will gradually wear out after years of usage, and it is useful forward planning to replace or refurbish such items when there is some spare money in the lodge fund, rather than having to raise a considerable amount of money for the emergency rectification of several items all at once. Lodges which present Past Masters' jewels to successive outgoing Masters will often purchase several at a time, and if your reserve is becoming depleted then you may have to take appropriate action.

Routine Correspondence

The correspondence file has been referred to above, and you are the focus of almost all correspondence that the lodge receives or sends. This will include items from and to Grand Lodge, Provincial Grand Lodge, the local Group, lodges meeting on the same premises and the Hall committee, the caterers, hotels, etc. If you hoard everything, then your correspondence files will grow at an alarming rate and, as a lot of the items do not necessarily have to be kept by you, the decision always has to be made as to what you retain and what you can eliminate, after bringing it to the attention of the lodge. If there is no other copy of the document in existence, for example a letter from a person expressing the wish to be made a Freemason, then this should be retained in the lodge archives. If it refers to money, then again as a rule of thumb it should be retained by you, the Treasurer or the Charity Steward in case there is a review of why subscriptions had to be set so high, etc. If there is a copy retained in other people's files, such as in the Provincial office, then after the appropriate response has been made your copy of the letter could be destroyed after a reasonable period of time has elapsed. Be aware that in this instance a response to the letter which will be retained in your files must have referred to the subject matter and date of issue, so that a copy of the relevant document can always be obtained at a future date if necessary. But circulars and summonses from other lodges sent to you out of courtesy can be disposed of after each event has happened.

Having dealt with eliminating what other people have sent to you, what about the correspondence that you are going to send to them and fill their files? There should be an established listing of recipients of the summons for each lodge meeting, with Province probably requesting several copies being sent to the Provincial Secretary or directly to the senior Officers of the Province. Local lodges and Group Officers may also receive a copy of all summonses, and you may additionally include your lodge newsletter so that they can keep abreast of developments in your lodge as they occur.

After each lodge meeting there will probably be a festive board, and you may have to inform the caterers in writing of your requirements in terms of the menu and numbers dining. If the meal following a special lodge meeting or for a social function is to be held in a location outside the Masonic Hall, there will be correspondence about the meal as well as confirming other details you have provisionally agreed with the venue. You may also book a table at the Provincial meeting, and remember to specify any special dietary needs that you are aware of as appropriate, but some time after the event all relevant correspondence could be disposed of.

Lodge Newsletter

The lodge members expect to receive the summons for each meeting and any information sent to you by Grand Lodge or Provincial Grand Lodge for distribution. They may also receive the lodge minutes and the Lodge Committee minutes if it is traditional to circulate them, so they are then fully conversant with the formal activities of the lodge. If you have several members living a distance away from the lodge meeting place, they will not necessarily be able to attend the lodge meetings as frequently as they may have done in the past. It might be an interesting project for the lodge to contemplate creating an informal newsletter, not necessarily for every meeting, so that all members can pick up snippets of news about their colleagues.

There are many things you can include in such a publication, though beware of straying onto Masonic proceedings in any detail (BoC177) and the Data Protection Act. Every new member can have a brief pen portrait inserted, with perhaps more detail than was included in the summons covering his ballot; his lady's name and those of any children and where they are schooling/working, etc., and possibly even a photograph. For existing members you can note any changes of address, perhaps as they leave work and move elsewhere for their retirement, and also any additions to their families as they occur. You can then include any information about special activities they have been involved in, such as parachute jumps or tackling Army assault courses for charity.

Very soon you may have a membership writing eagerly to you to inform their colleagues what they are doing in the world, whether by letter or e-mail, and telling you of their plans if they are going on a cruise or holidaying in some other exotic location. They may send you a report on how the holiday went and a picture of them swimming with dolphins or whatever. They might even include details of visiting lodges whilst away from home. Others may be reporting on winning some angling contests – hopefully not dwelling on the enormity of the ones that got away – and also on other sporting or recreational activities, as well as on competing in any Masonic events. Very soon you could have a newsletter that keeps the membership in contact with each other and one which is an enjoyable quarterly or half-yearly read about their friends and colleagues in their own Masonic family. It will allow you to warn them months or years in advance of major celebrations in the lodge, so that they can perhaps plan their holidays to be in the area for that occasion, and then the lodge family can be reunited to a greater extent than is the norm.

Your lodge may have one or two members, especially among the younger generation, who are computer wizards who may offer to compile the newsletter for you. And if their progression through the lodge is likely to take some time, why not involve them in a project that they can undertake probably more efficiently than the older lodge members, and at the same time let them feel they are making a significant contribution to the life of their lodge? Part of the enjoyment of lodge membership is in identifying and using the talents of various members for the benefit of all, and for the younger members it may also serve as a further introduction to some of the older members with whom they may not interact very often at lodge meetings.

Ceremonies for Other Lodges

As well as conferring degrees on the lodge members, a lodge can be requested to do so by other lodges. Such occasions arose many times during the First and Second World Wars, when large numbers of Armed Forces personnel were billeted considerable distances away from their homes and lodges for war duties, often at very short notice. If a Mason was an Initiate or a Fellowcraft and would be away from home for an undefined time, the Master of his mother lodge wrote to a lodge local to where the brother was billeted and asked it to perform the next degree(s) for him. Doubtless Provincial Grand Lodge would be made aware of what was going on, but this eventuality was already catered for in the rules (BoC173). This could even be done if the mother lodge were of a different Constitution, although on this occasion both Grand Lodges would be required to give their formal agreement. After such a degree was conferred, you as Secretary would have to inform the candidate's lodge and Grand Lodge of the date on which he was passed or raised as required.

Sometimes one lodge is inundated with candidates, while perhaps others in the same area have rarely seen candidates, so why is the pleasure of conducting the ceremonies not shared a little more? It would be a special event for the candidate to undergo a second or third degree in another lodge, and doubtless his friends and possibly his proposer and seconder could accompany him, or the Master may designate it an official visit to the other lodge and arrive with quite a retinue. It should not be difficult for the candidate's lodge to provide some of its members to perform parts of the ceremony, perhaps the obligation or the demonstrations of the signs (no foreign encroachment tolerated!), and it could provide a real fillip for the host lodge and possibly begin a closer and lasting friendship between the lodges.

Permanently Changing the Meeting Date or Place

The request for a dispensation to change the lodge meeting day or place for rare occasions has already been covered in the section on meetings, and if possible you should telephone the Provincial Secretary and advise him of your requirements. This enables you to receive his advice before you put pen to paper for the formal request, which will assist you in wording the letter, but some Provinces make a small charge for the dispensation, so remember to include the cheque with the letter – doubtless Province will bring this to your attention during your discussions. If the change of premises will be for several meetings, you will also be advised whether a dispensation can be granted to cover all of those meetings or a separate one for each is required.

Taking the scenario one step further, your lodge members may have decided to change when and/or where the lodge meets on a permanent basis. This will usually have been a thoroughly thought through decision over a period of months or longer, and for example you will need to agree to a transfer date with your current and new premises, and this may include crossing Provincial boundaries with the blessing of both Provinces. Many older lodges used to move their meeting place on a regular basis, but lodges nowadays tend to be more content with their current venues.

You will obviously have to amend your lodge bylaws to cover the required changes, and these will have to be detailed on the summons for the meeting following the proposition, so that the members can formally adopt the changes. The decision to move requires a two-thirds majority among the attendees. The new bylaws and a copy of the minutes when they were amended must then be sent to Grand Lodge via the Provincial Office for ratification before the move of date and/or place is made (BoC141-2). The new venue will have to be vetted as being suitable to hold Masonic meetings, so if you are not joining other lodges in an existing Hall, your proposed premises will have to be inspected by Province and declared acceptable.

Social Activities

Most lodges have some nights that are different from the routine. While the installation meeting is somewhat special, and normally has a larger than normal attendance, there may also be some light-hearted evenings such as Olde English Nights and Burns' Suppers for the brethren to enjoy. Hopefully there will be some assistance for the Secretary on and before the night, because there will be the entertainment to provide, either home-grown or booked to be delivered by others, a special menu, and selected fines, etc., to tempt some money from the brethren's pockets. There may be souvenir glasses or tankards to have engraved with the lodge and perhaps the Master's name, and you will need the booking forms returned well in advance to place the orders for the required number of items. A lodge sportsman's dinner would be organised along the same lines, with celebrity speakers invited to attract a larger number of Masons wanting to come to enjoy the event.

Many lodges include their ladies in their social activities, and perhaps your lodge has a social committee to oversee the various details. You as Secretary will be required to distribute if not also generate notices and booking forms for each of the events, and not just to your own lodge members but also to other lodges whose members might support you. Many lodges have Ladies' Evenings and socials, and some occasionally invite their wives or partners to a Ladies' Dining-In night, i.e. a "white table" meal to replace the all-male festive board after a lodge meeting. These are often held near Christmas, and you might organise a sherry reception for the ladies while you are having your lodge meeting. If you have more than one lodge room in the Masonic Hall, you may arrange a guided tour of the other room so that the ladies who are relatively new to the lodge gain a better appreciation of where their men disappear to on a monthly basis. For these, and any outside activities your lodge enjoys putting on, it will be down to you to oversee or assist in the organisational aspects, or to delegate your keen Assistant Secretary to do so.

Formal Lodge Celebrations

While the social side of the lodge is concerned with activities during most years, there are other special events that concern the lodge on the slightly more serious side. When a member achieves the milestone of 50 years in the Craft, many Provinces send a representative – often an Assistant Provincial Grand Master – to congratulate the celebrant at his anniversary meeting. Someone will be delegated to say a few words about the brother, and he will need information from your individual records on each member, so that he can accurately describe the early years as well as the more recent ones. You may also have to contact the Secretaries of any previous lodges to which the celebrant belonged, in order to compile a fuller perspective of his overall Masonic career. Apart from the visiting dignitaries to add lustre to the occasion, there may also be one or two special features added to the festive board in honour of the chief guest. Again, a quick call to the Provincial office will provide you with a useful framework to plan within, while you may well also try to locate members who left several years before to see if they can return for this special occasion, particularly if they were contemporaries of the celebrant.

For major lodge anniversaries there will again be some distinguished guests, especially for a lodge centenary, and Province will have a well-used and proven formula for such events. If the Provincial Grand Master is bringing all of his acting Officers, then there is likely to be a bumper attendance, and you may be forced to look for larger dining facilities than usual. The lodge will doubtless form a small committee in good time to help organise the event, as you and the Treasurer will not be able to cope on your own, and they will be wanting to look through the lodge records in order to update the lodge history. Perhaps it is intended to produce a bound volume or a smaller paper edition, but in order to fill in all of the required details the benefit of storing lodge records electronically will be very useful. You should be able to compile a list of Masters and senior lodge Officers throughout the additional years since the last lodge history, and you or somebody should be able to skim through the meetings each year to spot the highlights. To scan the minutes for more details will take more time, so it is useful to have a team sharing the work but, as with most things, you will find that everyone expects you to know everything that is happening or supposed to be happening.

Another special lodge meeting may be a banner dedication, whether for a new banner or a replacement one, although a refurbished banner cannot be rededicated. This is one time that the Provincial Chaplain could attend, and he will probably be accompanied by the Provincial Director of Ceremonies or one of his Deputies. Again Province will have a set routine to use as a framework for the ceremony, and advice should be sought at an early stage of the planning.

New Lodges

One of the reasons that there may be a banner dedication service is that the lodge is relatively new. Throughout the history of the English Constitution, lodges have started, operated, and then closed, just as previously operative masons had come together for major Medieval building projects and then disbanded once the work had been completed. There have been periods of time when there has been an explosion in new lodges, for example after the two World Wars, but there has recently been a significant slowing down in the number of new lodges being consecrated each year. Most Provinces now have Installed Masters' lodges, and also Provincial Officers' and Charity Stewards' lodges, and currently there seem to be numerous daylight or lunchtime lodges springing up, as well as a few standard Craft lodges.

As with many other aspects of Masonry, the Provincial office will be able to provide you with advice on the steps you have to take *en route* to forming a new lodge (BoC94-100). If you are to be the Founding Secretary you will have a large number of interactions to deal with, and you need to start with a core of at least seven brethren who are like-minded in what they wish to achieve (BoC94). The Provincial Secretary will arrange a meeting with himself, or with the local Group Officers in the area where you are proposing to hold your meetings, to assess the business case for the lodge – with decreasing memberships in existing lodges, there is no point in starting another lodge for what could be only a limited lifetime.

You and your colleagues will need to talk with the existing local lodges, not least to allay any fears that you will be in competition with them for attracting new members, and to determine from the Masonic Hall what days are available for the new lodge to use. You then have to decide on which days you will meet and how frequently, what regalia you will need to obtain and what the Hall can provide, what form of ritual you will follow, when your lodge year will begin and end, and what Founders' fees you will need to levy to cover the costs. Do not forget that Grand Lodge charges a considerable sum for a new warrant, which remains the property of the Grand Master (BoC101-3), and there will be a banquet after the Consecration meeting with several guests to provide meals for. You will need to assess the accommodation for both the meeting and the eating, and decide how many guests each Founder can invite if there is a limit to how many can be comfortably catered for.

The Treasurer designate can take care of gathering in the various monies, but you have to obtain a petition form from the Grand Secretary via the Province, and fill in the details of all of the Founders, who should normally all be Master Masons of at least three years' standing. They in turn will need to obtain clearance certificates from every lodge of which they are currently or ever have been a member, and also to sign the petition. The Founders need to agree who are to be the Principal Officers (BoC97) and the other four brethren to be named on the warrant. You then need to arrange with your sponsoring lodge that its Principal Officers will sign the petition in open lodge at the meeting where the vote is to be taken to support the creation of the new lodge, and some of your Founders may wish to attend in order to witness the first formal birth pangs of your lodge (BoC94). The completed petition and all of the clearance certificates you now send to the Provincial Secretary for him to transmit to the Grand Secretary, and the petition will be formally accepted at a meeting of Grand Lodge.

You now arrange with Province when the consecration day will be, which may not be on what will be your normal lodge meeting day, and agree with the caterers the menu for the meal and perhaps arrange for a welcoming snack for attendees of the meeting, some of whom may have travelled a long way. You then need to agree with the Provincial Director of Ceremonies how many and when the rehearsals will be held, as these will involve the Founders and the acting Provincial Officers. You may also have some candidates to propose, either as initiates or as joining members, and you require all of their details and the forms completed; and then you send out the invitations and collect the consecration booklet you have managed to create in your spare time!

Ageing Lodges

At the other end of the spectrum, there is the lodge that is struggling to stay alive. You may find that as the lodge membership decreases, although you nominally still have several members on the books, some are too infirm to attend meetings, some live too far away to attend every meeting, and with only a hard core of members filling the offices at the regular lodge meetings you are perhaps already having to invite visitors to assist you. It is stated that if there are less than five members on the Grand Lodge annual return, the lodge has to cease to meet (BoC188-90), although difficulties will have been encountered before this level of membership, because each lodge requires nine regular Officers. As no member can hold more than one regular office, and only the Tyler can be an elected non-member, it seems that less than eight members would also cause problems at the installation meeting (BoC104). Interestingly even with less than five members the Grand Master can grant a dispensation for the lodge to continue to meet, in order for it to sort out if it has a future or not (BoC188). It is also notable that some major decisions in the life of a lodge – moving premises, or excluding a member – require a two-thirds majority, but others such as the decision of a lodge to petition for a new lodge, and the vote by members to terminate their own lodge, require only more than half of the people present to concur.

In olden times lodges had no option but to hand in their warrants if they could not continue, although it was not uncommon for a lodge to perhaps reinvent itself as a lunchtime lodge to stay in existence. Occasionally the members of a lodge returned their warrant and joined another lodge *en masse*, and a favourite over the years has been for a daughter lodge to be absorbed back into the mother lodge whence it came. Recently another option has been made available, which is to amalgamate lodges, and the idea is to create a strong lodge where two or more weak lodges have decided to join forces (BoC102A). It obviously works best if the lodges have been interacting for some time, perhaps enjoying combined socials so that the numbers at each event are not too low, and Provinces and their Groups will know which lodges are contemplating this course of action. The Group or Province will arrange a meeting with each lodge so that the members are aware of the ramifications of amalgamation, and they can discuss all of the options open to them. The lodges then need to talk together, perhaps in a working party with the representatives of each lodge being able to report back on the progress achieved during the discussions. The lodges will need to vote separately on a formal proposition of a course of action and, if all of the votes are in favour, they can work together towards amalgamation. The voting requirements are different for the various lodges; the receiving lodge – the one that will be embracing the other lodge(s) – requires a two-thirds majority to accept them, but the incoming lodges only need to exceed half.

The amalgamation may be timed to coincide with an installation meeting, when the lodges can agree between themselves who are to be the new Officers in the amalgamated lodge, and Province or Group will arrange for the appropriate ceremonial details to be available for the rehearsal meetings. Perhaps it is you as the lodge Secretary who will be ceasing operations, and you will provide your membership list and other lodge records so that the new Secretary can combine all of the relevant records together. At the ceremony the redundant warrants can be handed over to the Provincial representative for onward transmission to Grand Lodge to be cancelled and then returned to be kept with the new warrant, which will have been presented to the first Master of the amalgamated lodge. You may be asked to ensure that all of your other lodge records, Minute Books, etc., are sent to Province for safe keeping before finally being archived at Grand Lodge, and you may decide to update your lodge history so its own story from cradle to grave can be recorded for posterity.

As well as archiving your lodge records, your members will need clearance certificates to say they were in good standing when the lodge closed, and any Entered Apprentices and Fellowcrafts will need interim certificates before they continue their Masonic careers in new lodges. You may have regalia and additional funds to dispose of. The lodge that many members are joining may require some of its regalia replacing, so access to yours may be opportune, otherwise perhaps a new lodge is starting somewhere near you and would appreciate any assistance in defraying the cost of setting up. Although it is strictly a matter for the lodge Treasurer, if you have any funds left after all outstanding bills and dues have been paid, you may elect to transfer them to the receiving lodge in the amalgamation, because it will hopefully be looking after any of your lodge dependants such as widows in the future. Otherwise you may consider transferring the funds to a Group or Provincial fund, if it has been agreed that the Group or Provincial Almoner respectively will be ensuring a continuity of care once your lodge has ceased to exist.

Aspects of the Rules (concerning Other Routine and Non-Routine Matters)

BoC94 – a Grand Lodge petition form for a new lodge must be signed by at least seven petitioning Master Masons; signed in open lodge by the Master and Wardens of the sponsoring lodge after a majority of members of that lodge at the meeting have voted in favour (abstentions count as votes against); and forwarded to the Grand Secretary via the Provincial Grand Secretary, together with proof of good standing from every lodge of which each petitioner is or has been a member.

BoC97 – each new lodge shall be constituted by the Grand Master or a Past Master whom he has appointed, and only the Master and Wardens named in the warrant can be installed and invested respectively.

BoC100 – a lodge new to the Province, by creation or joining, is placed at the bottom of the list of lodges in the Province.

BoC101-3 – every lodge requires a warrant of constitution in order to meet; it remains the property of the Grand Master and is given into the charge of each new Master at his installation; and if the warrant is lost the lodge must suspend further meetings until a warrant of confirmation is received from the Grand Master.

BoC102A – if two or more lodges wish to amalgamate, the Grand Master may at his discretion grant a Certificate of Amalgamation.

BoC128 – all lodges held within 5 miles of Freemasons' Hall are London lodges.

BoC129 – all lodges further than 10 miles from Freemasons' Hall are in Provinces or Districts, while lodges 5-10 miles from the Hall may be either London or Provincial lodges.

BoC136 – model bylaws are available from Grand Lodge, but each lodge can frame its own bylaws; however, the bylaws and any amendments shall be approved by the Provincial Grand Master.

BoC137 – lodge bylaws shall specify the regular days and meeting place of the lodge, the regular meeting for the elections and the subsequent installation meeting.

BoC138 – every member shall be given a copy of the bylaws, and a copy be given to each Master at his installation, and their acceptance agrees compliance with them.

BoC141 – the removal of a lodge to, from or within a Province requires the prior consent of the Provincial Grand Master(s) as well as the Grand Master, and in the vote in lodge at least two-thirds of those present have to vote in favour of the move.

BoC143 – while in office, the Master and Wardens own in trust all the property of the lodge not already vested with named trustees.

BoC154 – in its bylaws a lodge may constitute a committee to consider and report on proposals for membership, and it or another committee may address any other matters by resolution of the lodge; the Master *ex officio* is entitled to preside over every committee of the lodge.

BoC173 – one lodge may pass or raise a brother from another lodge on the written request of the Master of that brother's lodge and, if from another Grand Lodge, this will be countersigned by the brother's Grand Secretary through the conferring lodge's Grand Secretary; and after the degree the conferring lodge's Secretary shall forward to the brother's lodge (via the Grand Secretaries if required) certification of when the degree was conferred.

BoC188-90 – when the number of lodge members on the Grand Lodge return is less than five, the lodge shall cease to exist and the lodge warrant and papers be returned to the Grand Master, although he may grant a dispensation for the members to continue to meet until he has decided whether the lodge should be continued or erased; and if a lodge should fail to meet for one year, it is liable to be erased.

Retirement and the Assistant Secretary

So just when you have developed a real feel for the job, and have read the Book of Constitutions so many times you can quote whole paragraphs *verbatim*, you or the lodge decide you have had enough. If the lodge tradition is that someone enjoys all the fun of being a Secretary for only three to five years, then that was understood when you took on the job. However, in many lodges there are few volunteers for taking on the office, and some Secretaries soldier on for many more years than they initially envisaged, probably still enjoying aspects of the work and possibly now a little more adept at delegating some of the work which can be shared.

If you are retiring by mutual agreement with the lodge, then your successor is probably already lined up. Always remember the excuse from business management – "we can only promote you when we find a replacement for the job you are leaving behind", so you may need to find your own successor. When it is understood that a person's future position and salary at work depends on finding someone suitable to take his place, it normally galvanises that person into rapid action. But assuming that there is someone who is keen to try his hand at the office, you can suggest that he becomes your Assistant Secretary, though if your lodge has made that office a progressive one for juniors so that they learn a little about the lodge organisation, this course of action will not be possible.

Whether you have a junior or successor as Assistant Secretary, as suggested by the title, he is there to assist you as required, but you should give some thought as to how you will interact together. If you ask him merely to shadow all the work you do, then he will be very useful when you cannot be present at a meeting for any reason, but without some specific responsibilities he may feel that most of the time he is not necessarily serving a worthwhile purpose. Some lodges delegate the duties of the organising and minute-taking of Lodge Committees to the Assistant Secretary; others make it his duty to read out the lodge minutes at every meeting (assuming that your penmanship is legible); a few lodges make him the unofficial prompter in the ceremonies, and also allow him to organise the meals after lodge meetings. And if your successor has a few spare evenings, you can suggest he reads the Book of Constitutions that will become his bible just as much as it was yours.

Once your successor has been appointed and invested, perhaps you will be given the chance to address him on his duties. And many of the best informal such addresses are when a predecessor warns the new Officer of some of the pitfalls awaiting him: "Now you are wearing that collar, I feel as though a great weight has been lifted..." You may for a time feel somewhat like a policeman, never totally off duty, and you will always be there or at the end of a telephone if your successor needs some quick advice on how to proceed. But in all likelihood he will go from strength to strength, and you can enjoy life as a backbencher, or return to performing some of the lodge ceremonial, or even take the time to concentrate on some side degree activities that you have postponed for a while. You will hopefully have memories of a job well done, much appreciated by your lodge and Province, and also of having helped a great many people in the Craft to enjoy their Masonry.

Appendices

A Checklist for the Content of the Summons

In order to establish a framework for discussing the different items on the summons, it is assumed that a folded four-page variant has been adopted. Check your lodge summons carefully for other items, as this list is not necessarily comprehensive.

First Page
Lodge name and number – the numbers have not been changed since 1863, although with now about 12% of the lodges having lapsed, closing up the numbers may be countenanced one day – perhaps as we near 10,000 lodges on the list.
Town in which the lodge meets – lodges move around less than before, and even then it was usually between almost adjacent hostelries rather than any great distance.
Province in which the lodge meets – except when lodges are meeting close to the borders of adjacent Provinces, it is even rarer for lodges to move between Provinces.
Lodge warrant and consecration dates – these are unlikely to change.
Lodge logo or picture – this can change as a new banner or logo may be created, although all banner and badge designs must be approved by Grand Lodge.
Lodge being the patron of a particular charity or Festival – for a Masonic charity your patronage may be long-lived, but with a Provincial Festival the patronage should be eliminated either when the Festival is ended or at least when a new Festival is started.

Second Page
List of lodge Officers and representatives for the current year – these may almost all

change after the installation meeting, but the elections of some representatives may be held at a time of year different from the business or installation meeting.

Addresses and telephone numbers of various lodge Officers – as the Officers change, obviously the contact details will have to be changed, and if they are ex-directory check with the people that they are happy for the number to be listed in a summons.

Address and telephone number of the meeting place – probably well-known to members, but may be of great use to visitors who receive a summons, particularly if they are held up in traffic, etc., on their way to the meeting.

Contact information of Group Officers – again check that the people are happy for ex-directory numbers to be printed.

Almoner to be informed if any member or one of his family is indisposed – with appropriate wording, this can remain unchanged even when the Almoner changes.

Request for members to inform the Secretary of any change of address – normally no change is necessary.

Reminder to book meals in good time – normally no change is necessary.

Reminder that lodge subscriptions are due – this may be a temporary feature part-way through the subscription year if the Treasurer wants to issue a gentle reminder, before the more heavy-handed treatment is instigated.

Statement that Royal Arch is a continuation of the Third Degree and contact names – obviously unlikely to change unless the contact changes.

Warning that visiting lodges overseas should be referred to Grand Lodge – unlikely to require alteration.

Antient Charge about the importance of attendance at lodge – no change necessary.

Quote from Dr Oliver about keeping lodge membership select – no requirement for change, unless another quotation is proposed.

Third Page

Sentence from Secretary convening the meeting at the request of the Master, detailing the date, time and place of the meeting, and Secretary's name – the date will change with every meeting, the time infrequently, and the place unlikely; Secretary's details alter with change of Officer; be especially careful if you are in a lunar lodge, as many diaries do not include phases of the moon.

Code of dress recommended for the meeting – this may change for installations and special meetings, requiring more formal dress; it would be a courtesy to those who do not possess formal attire to include the phrase "…or dark suit" in any rewording.

Noting any dignitaries who are attending – these are only likely to be included for special occasions and for the installation, for example the Provincial Grand Master's representative; ensure their ranks are correct, especially after a recent promotion, or they may be offended.

Noting at what time the toast to absent brethren will be honoured – this may alter for the installation, especially if the meeting moves to a Saturday for example and starts much earlier than the standard lodge meeting.

Notice of the dates of practice and Lodge Committee meetings – as the lodge meeting date changes, so these will; be especially careful with the installation practices, as you may have additional ones; and be careful with meetings close to Bank Holidays, as you may have to adjust the meeting dates to avoid these.

Notice of coming Provincial meeting – this will obviously be a regular annual or bi-annual event, and may therefore only be included intermittently; be aware that it may impact on your lodge, practice or committee meetings.

List of business to be transacted at the meeting – this obviously varies for every meeting, and the business meeting and the installation meeting will have very different agendas from the others.

Details of people to be balloted for – this includes full names and addresses, ages and/or dates of birth, full descriptions of occupations and places of business, membership of other lodges, proposers and seconders and at which lodge meetings they were put forward.

List of brethren waiting to go through higher degrees – these will obviously change as the lodge works its way through the series of ceremonies for each brother in turn.

List of dates of future lodge meetings – check yours and the Masonic Hall's diaries for advanced meetings, especially if yours is a lunar lodge, or one of your meetings falls close to Christmas or Easter; the latter can vary from mid-March to the end of April.

Statement about meeting happily – unlikely to change; may you always meet happily.

Fourth Page

List of lodge Founders – the list will not change after the consecration, but you may traditionally continue updating the rank to which each has been promoted until his death, when there should be no further change.

List of Past Masters of the lodge – this increases with every installation, but again you may be updating each individual's rank after he has retired from the Chair, and this exercise could be performed once a year after the installation, or also after each Grand Lodge investiture and Provincial Grand Lodge meeting if preferred.

Annotation for which of the Founders and Past Masters has resigned or died – the same problem arises as with updating ranks.

List of Past Masters of other lodges who are members of the lodge – this may be courtesy to those who have joined the lodge from other lodges, perhaps when people move jobs or retire to other parts of the country, and again you may need to update their ranks (and they may have gained honours from other Provinces, so their promotions will not be listed by your lodge's indigenous Province), and they will be removed from the list only when they resign or die.

List of honorary members of the lodge – these may include senior Provincial Officers who are non-members, and their ranks need updating as they are promoted by Grand Lodge; otherwise the only change will be the removal of their names when they die.

Mourning – note that Grand Lodge or Provincial Grand Lodge may specify a period of mourning to be observed as a mark of respect after the death of a senior Mason, and one of the requirements may be during that time to print the summons in black if it is normally coloured, or to be edged within a black border if it is normally black.

List of Provincial Officers and Other Dignitaries (with salutes)

Senior Grand Officers
MW Grand Master (11)
MW Pro Grand Master (11)
RW Deputy Grand Master (9)
RW Assistant Grand Master (9)
RW Grand Wardens (7)

Grand Ranks with the title of Very Worshipful are from Chaplain to Grand Superintendent of Works, and they merit 5 salutations; the rest merit 3 (BoC6)

Provincial Grand Officers
RW Provincial Grand Master (7)
RW Pro Provincial Grand Master (7)
(V)W Deputy Provincial Grand Master (5)*
Assistant Provincial Grand Master (5)*
Senior Warden
Junior Warden
(V)W Chaplain (5 if V)**
Treasurer (elected, not appointed)
Registrar
Secretary
Director of Ceremonies
Sword Bearer
Superintendent of Works
Deputy Chaplain
Deputy Registrar
Deputy Secretary
Deputy Director of Ceremonies
Deputy Sword Bearer
Deputy Superintendent of Works

Almoner
Charity Steward
Senior Deacon
Junior Deacon
Assistant Chaplain
Assistant Registrar
Assistant Secretary
Assistant Director of Ceremonies
Assistant Sword Bearer
Assistant Superintendent of Works
Organist
Standard Bearer
Assistant Standard Bearer
Deputy Organist
Pursuivant
Assistant Pursuivant
Steward
Tyler

N.B. three salutations unless otherwise designated.

* Deputy and Assistant Provincial Grand Masters receive 5 only in their Province, Past Deputies and Assistants receive 5 if they had more than 2 years in office (BoC6); however, if they are Very Worshipful, they will receive 5 in any Province.

Other Officers
Group Chairman
Deputy Group Chairman
Group Treasurer
Group Secretary
Group Almoner
Group Information (Press) Officer

Provincial Information (Press) Officer

Salutations will be as merited by Grand or Provincial Grand Ranks

The Lodge
Director of
Ceremonies

Introduction

At the start of the Secretary's section, Rudyard Kipling's listing of his serving-men, "What and Why and When and How and Where and Who", was inserted. If these questions are applicable to the Secretary, then they are even more applicable to the Director of Ceremonies. With regard to all of the ceremonies that he will be trying to organise throughout the year, he will need to know *what* ceremony is being worked, *when* it will be performed, the lodge traditions for *how* exactly it will be conducted and *where*abouts in the lodge room and by *whom*. From the junior members in particular, he will doubtless be inundated with questions as to *why* the different parts of the ceremony are performed in these ways, *what* significance they have, and historically *how* they arose, and so on.

It has already been said that the Director of Ceremonies is somewhat like a team coach, always in full control of whatever is happening, but operating and encouraging largely in the background. The team squad has discussed and talked through the game plan at length, and during the game the coach might have to resort to one or two signals or even brief verbal instructions/reminders – in American football some team players have microphones and speakers in their helmets so that a private word can suffice, but as yet neither English association or rugby football club players wear such helmets, and neither normally do Masons in lodges, so sometimes the communications will have to be visible and audible to all those present.

Unlike the Secretary, which is a "regular" and therefore mandatory office in the lodge, the Director of Ceremonies is an "additional" office and not mandatory. Despite this, few lodges choose to manage without one. Whereas the Secretary has the dual-purpose role of internally looking after the lodge members and externally conducting any formal liaison with outside bodies interacting with the lodge, the role of the Director of Ceremonies is almost totally introspective. His parish is exclusively within the precincts of the lodge, and he ensures that everything that happens in a lodge meeting and at the subsequent meal is performed exactly as it should be. This means he has to be able to maintain the traditions required by the lodge, but also has to ensure that the meetings conform to the expectations of the Masonic hierarchy. This will include the Province in which the lodge resides as well as the more local Group requirements, because from time to time there will be external visitors who will report back if they see anything that they deem to be untoward.

On being invested, the Director of Ceremonies is informed that he is required to see that all of the ceremonies are properly conducted, that visitors and brethren are placed as befits their rank, and that the lodge Officers are situated correctly around the lodge room – and this includes the temporary substitutes if any invested Officers are not able to be present. In addition to these aspects, we might first assess what characteristics could be useful in a Director of Ceremonies.

Personal
Attributes

It is probable that you have already aspired to this office before the lodge has asked you to consider taking it on; this is certainly not an office that should be forced on anyone against his own inclination. You will have a reasonable understanding of the Craft ceremonies, and will undoubtedly have taken part in aspects of each of them; in fact you will have probably progressed through a series of offices within the lodge.

You are probably a Past Master of this or another lodge and, in holding that office, you will already have interacted closely with your own Director of Ceremonies. You will possibly have thought to yourself what an excellent support he was during your year in the Chair. So think about the qualities in him that you admired, and check yourself for similar ones; this is another case of the Wardens' address at the installation: "What you find praiseworthy in others, you should carefully imitate, and what in them may appear defective, you should in yourselves amend." There is nothing wrong in copying role models, because as the head of the Sony Corporation once said about the "Walkman" clones: "Imitation is the sincerest form of flattery."

But enough of quotes. It will be useful if you are a Past Master, because otherwise you will miss the inner workings of the installation ceremony, and this is just one of the occasions that is likely to run more smoothly with you shepherding things along. You will also be reasonably proficient in the lodge ritual, because this will give you the confidence to advise others, whether by prompting when appropriate or in guiding someone along his own learning path. There is much to be said for being able to lead from the front and being able to deliver all of the ceremonies as required without much warning, and such inherent capability will enable you to go about your duties confidently, but it is not all that is required in this job. I remain unconvinced that the Director of Ceremonies needs to be the best ritualist in the lodge *per se*, just as the best football managers and coaches have not necessarily been the top international players in the earlier stages of their careers.

You will require a clear speaking voice. While a whispering Director of Ceremonies can operate adequately in some lodges, a modicum of extra volume will assist in persuading the brethren to quieten down and listen to you. And it is surprising how quickly the human voice can be absorbed in a lodge room or at the festive board. The bodies, clothes, and the furnishings such as the carpets, seats, banners and other wall coverings, etc., can make a human voice unprojectable beyond surprisingly short distances. This is not to say you need a Sergeant Major's stentorian capability, but some volume certainly. And clarity is required at any volume, as well as being able to speak at a controlled pace, rather than being word-perfect and gabbling through your announcement so that no-one is any the wiser as to what you were trying to say. You will have seen many brethren delivering parts of the ritual and other items in different ways, from the excellent to the less so, and you will therefore know what works well and otherwise. Just as your speaking style may well be an example for the brethren to copy, your standard of dress should also set the standard for the lodge; the white gloves should be clean and the black shoes clean and polished – and preferably avoid using the first to polish the second! And you will need to make carrying your wand look as if you were born with it in your hand, because it will be with you for almost everything except when leading the salutations.

It is useful if you have a naturally erect posture (you were told as an Entered Apprentice to stand perfectly erect), as you need a confident if not necessarily a commanding stature when you move around the lodge room. That is not to say you should convey a forbidding presence, but rather by your own calm dignity you will be able to inspire calmness and confidence in those you escort; for some junior members perhaps performing their first pieces of ritual inside a full lodge room such inspiration will be most welcome. If the Director of Ceremonies appears to be in control of the situation, even when merely walking across the room to escort someone, it can become infectious by reassuring others and instilling confidence into them. Also unflappability certainly helps when awkward situations arise, such as the Master splitting his trousers at an elevating moment in the Third Degree, as has occurred more than once during my observations of the ceremonies.

However, perhaps more important than being personally able and skilled in the lodge ritual, you will need to be someone who can work with people. The lodge has made you the Director of Ceremonies in order to preserve the lodge traditions, not by you performing every aspect faultlessly, but by ensuring that every member is fully conversant with the correct way of doing things, from the simplest salutes to the longest pieces of prose. This will require something else from you: time and patience, and to be able to work with and advise others, at the lodge practices and on other occasions, will undoubtedly take a great deal of both.

Before leaving the relevant attributes, it might be worth giving some thought to prompting. It is of course very useful if you as the Director of Ceremonies can immediately produce the perfect prompt at any stage of any ceremony, but even the best of us can be caught out sometimes, and it does not look well for you to be thumbing through or even having an open ritual book on your lap. If you have lots of volunteers around the room, then the prompting from discreetly hidden books can be local to wherever the ceremony is currently taking place. You may delegate the Immediate Past Master to prompt the Master if required; otherwise the Secretary's table is the one place in the lodge room where papers are being spread out and organised for the various communications, etc., to be reported, and a prompt sheet or book here would not look out of place. It may be that the Secretary, the Treasurer or the Assistant Secretary can be quietly following the written script, and if for any reason you are temporarily stuck for a prompt, then a quick glance from you across the room should elicit the appropriate response. And the correctness of the assistance is all-important, because a wrong prompt can cause all sorts of confusion in the mind of the recipient, and completely jumble up the rest of the presentation, and is also an argument for only having a single prompt at any time, rather than well-intentioned helpers delivering a variety of different suggestions for the recipient to cope with.

As well as dealing with the pregnant pauses that can occur during the ceremonies, you also have another job which is harder to define. If the delivery of a piece of ritual is not word-perfect, how far off the correct version do you allow it to drift before bringing it back onto the correct track? You will need an appreciation for the importance of what is taking place; perhaps in an obligation there should be less latitude given than in the other parts of the ceremonies. This is a difficult call to make, and as a general rule it is perhaps better to let someone continue in full flow even if he is not 100% accurate. Just as with an incorrect prompt, an interruption can equally cause confusion, and the person delivering the piece of ritual may become disoriented and lose the thread of what he was saying. So you might assess what is important to the candidate, who would clearly benefit from a coherent presentation, and you could correct parts of the obligations as necessary, but allow slight deviations in the explanations of the tracing boards, etc., to go uncorrected if the gist of the story is there and intelligible. It is a personal call, and one you will find useful to try out in the lodge practices as well as in the proper ceremonies, and one you might discuss afterwards with your predecessor. In any event, stay calm and unflappable, trust your instincts, and the lodge will go along with you. Of course, what people do not realise is that, despite the calm exterior, you are probably churning over inside just as much as the more openly nervous ones, and fervently hoping that everything goes right.

To assist you in your quest for enlightenment, several Provinces organise workshops for lodge Directors of Ceremonies, not only to outline methods of coping with these kinds of problems, but also to reinforce the Provincial protocol when receiving dignitaries, etc., so if possible make the most of any opportunities that are presented to you. And it is worth noting that Provincial Directors of Ceremonies do not grow on trees – or indeed have other than normal parentage – but they and their Deputies are gleaned from the lodge equivalents across the Province, so if you have any aspirations in this direction, then the workshops are definitely useful training grounds in order to understand the Provincial protocol *in toto*.

Man Management

The Director of Ceremonies has usually been appointed because he is seen to be capable of maintaining the lodge traditions, which may include the excellence of the ritual performed, but he should always make the needs of the individual of greater importance. There is surely no point in trying to force someone, clearly struggling with one page of ritual, to have to deliver the six-page charge to a candidate after initiation; sharing out the work should be considered, and try to tailor the task to the capabilities of the individual concerned. If the main aim of the ceremony is for the candidate to learn more about what he has just undergone, does it matter that two or more people deliver the piece of ritual to him? This sharing of the work enables the member with more limited ability to feel he is still contributing positively to the lodge business whilst not over-effacing him.

Undoubtedly it would make the Director of Ceremonies' job very much easier if every Master in turn were a capable ritualist, but if the reverse were the case, should this prevent that member from becoming Master of the lodge? The early designers of the Masonic ritual and the sequencing of Officers were quite astute; the holding of each office from Inner Guard to Senior Warden progressively builds up the capability and confidence of the brother as a training course for being the Master of the lodge. Every credit to those lodges who have and regularly attain high standards in Masonic ritual, and manage to inspire successive Masters to perform well, but in other lodges how many brethren have been put off ever starting to progress towards the Chair of King Solomon by being told that they will have to be able to conduct all three degree ceremonies and the installation ceremony as a basic requirement of being Master? After all, the brethren of the lodge will collectively vote to appoint a Master Elect, and by doing so will be confirming their support for the person they have elected; to assist him in his year as Master, perhaps sharing out the work, may be one of the ways in which they can demonstrate that support.

Encouragement is the key to success. Even from being little boys, each of us has usually responded positively to praise and negatively to criticism, and some things do not change as you grow older. As you successfully achieve one goal, you automatically re-adjust your sights to higher attainments and, if you have been pleasantly surprised by what you have managed to achieve, you will want to keep surprising yourself. By doing so, you are also complying with the request levelled at you in the charge after your initiation: "...endeavour to make a daily advancement in Masonic knowledge". So the person who starts out with perhaps somewhat limited capabilities can with time and encouragement develop into being able to perform the required ritual satisfactorily. He may not actually enjoy the work it entails because it does not come naturally to him, but he will achieve a quiet satisfaction of a job done to the best of his abilities, probably surpassing his own expectations at the outset, and perhaps even yours.

What Each Officer Wants from You

You will know that any ceremony is a team effort, from the Tyler preparing the candidate, the Inner Guard admitting him, the Deacons escorting him, the Wardens questioning him, and the Master obligating him, and perhaps others joining in with additional aspects of the ceremony. It is obvious that you cannot personally carry out every role, and you have to entrust most if not all aspects of the ceremony to the appointed Officers or their stand-ins. So what advice will be most helpful to them? This is where you need to know each person as an individual; his strengths, his weaknesses, and his overall capabilities – this is one reason why the Director of Ceremonies is usually someone who has been a member of the lodge for a considerable time, so that he knows and is known by all of the members.

Probably the first advice for each Officer is to read the whole ceremony thoroughly in his ritual book, concentrating on the times when he is interacting with the candidate and other Officers. He needs to know the words correctly, and also know the questions or answers that follow in the various colloquies, and that in themselves prompt a further interchange. He will also be aware that whatever he says has to be audible, usually to everyone in the room, sometimes as a stage whisper to the candidate, and therefore he needs to enunciate clearly in order to be understood. Although those who are not used to public speaking may find it difficult at first, a slow delivery of words will be more easily heard than a rapid-fire one, especially with the furnishings of lodge rooms tending to absorb the human voice.

The Officers will also need to know what actions are required and when, because parts of the ceremonies have a visual impact as well as an audible one, on both the candidate and other attendees. Equally important to the Officers is to be reminded how the lodge copes with those less formal parts of the meetings outside the ceremonies. Each lodge will have its own style of opening and closing, and of performing all of the other items on the agenda, but rarely are they all written down in a ritual book, let alone in an Emulation or other standard version. Possibly the previous incumbent will have made notes to cover these aspects, and he may give you a copy of them to help you along the first few meetings until you have assimilated the role you have taken on.

A *résumé* of the various aspects on which the Officers will probably want advice is given in the Appendix, but the key person who needs your support is the one who appointed you, the Master. For the remainder of his installation meeting and for the bulk of the next lodge meeting, everything is new to him, and yet frequently Directors of Ceremonies do not take sufficient time to go through the whole running agenda of a meeting with a new Master. His copies of the first few summonses are likely to be covered with additional notes, as indeed yours will be to some extent for every meeting, as reminders of what is required and when. With the idea of helping the Master, some lodges seat the Director of Ceremonies next to him, rather than relying solely on the Immediate Past Master, so that there can be quiet words of guidance available throughout the meeting to cater for every situation.

If other lodge members are also taking part in the ceremonies, they also will need to know where they are required to be and when. If they are to be escorted it is quite easy: you will take them to where they need to be. If they are to make their own way across the lodge room, then it is also simple: they go to stand in front of the candidate ready to address him. If two or three brethren are delivering an item between them, perhaps one of the tracing boards, then they each make their own way forward in turn to deliver their respective parts, and the only request you may make is that they perhaps sit next to each other, so that it takes on the appearance of well-rehearsed team members each coming off the bench in turn during a game.

Practice Meetings
The best training ground for lodge members to test their memories and capabilities is the lodge practice. Some lodges hold one before each meeting, others may hold two or more (especially before an installation), and it is at these practices that the Director of Ceremonies discovers whether he is heading for a perfect or difficult ceremony at the following lodge meeting. This is also the time to take some corrective action if it looks like the latter, and remember that learning the Masonic ritual takes place in two different spheres of life: firstly the learning is mainly done individually in private, not in public as when reciting the times tables in school. Secondly the choreography of how to arrive at the appropriate place to deliver the next phase of the ceremony is where the public practice has most to offer, when juniors can run through the routine movements and interactions in the lodge – and can take on different roles at each practice – so that they begin to assimilate the flow of the ceremonial in the lodge. If you have candidates or are going to perform a

demonstration ceremony at a lodge meeting, then the immediately prior practice is likely to be performed by the same Officers in the practice as will shortly be operating in lodge. To make it more representative of the coming ceremony, you might bring out the lodge regalia to make it a dress rehearsal, even killing the lights if the ceremony is a third. Other lodge members can substitute for any Officers that are absent, and this is a useful way of allowing juniors to occupy the vacant posts and gain experience of participating in a ceremony from inside the team rather than merely watching as interested spectators.

If the practice is conducted without any sign of a ritual book, except from where the prompting is to be given, then by attempting to deliver their parts from memory you and the Officers can see how near perfection each of them is. You will all need to agree a signalling system that solicits a prompt only when required. When delivering the charge after initiation for the first time in lodge, at the prior practice I requested a prompt only if I looked round for one, otherwise I would be pausing for breath. At the practice my pauses after each paragraph became longer and longer to emphasise the point, but no prompts were forthcoming as they were not needed. In the lodge meeting the pauses were strictly for breath and shorter in duration than at the practice, but I felt confident that I would not be immediately assailed by a salvo of well-intentioned prompts from around the room at each intake of breath. It is a system that I have seen adopted successfully in many lodges and seems to work well, but there may be other methods that your lodge has found to be suitable for its needs, so use them. Ensure that everyone understands your system, and also that there is only one prompt, from you or the official prompter, rather than a multiplicity of them.

If some members are struggling to cope with their parts, they should perhaps have informed you before the final practice, but what do you do in this situation? After the practice session you might take the Officer to one side and discuss how best to make the necessary improvements. If a Deacon is not sure about the perambulations and positioning the candidate, then let him walk through his steps with you as the candidate a couple of times so that he builds up more confidence about where to be and how to arrive there. If remembering the words is problematical, then check if he has the time to read the different sections again over the next few days, and try to arrange for you or the ADC or another colleague to visit him at home in order to quickly run through the items again. You might also ask an experienced colleague to sit near the Officer during the lodge meeting, so that there is support nearby if it is required. And often it is remembering the first words of a paragraph that is the problem, and a quiet and timely prompt will trigger the required continuation and would hardly be noticed by others during the ceremony.

In one of my lodges we had a Master who had not found the ritual easy to cope with during his progression through the various offices in the lodge, and wanted an additional practice for his own benefit. The other Officers who were able to attend met at his house between the two lodge practices, and he went through the parts of the ceremony quietly and with increasing confidence, and in all of his subsequent ceremonies he acquitted himself very well. On these occasions the lodge Director of Ceremonies was never present, as only the junior Officers attended, but I am sure that he was kept up to date on how things were going and would have assisted further if he had thought it necessary.

If you are one of those lodges that holds more than one practice per lodge meeting, then you may call one the junior practice and another the senior practice. The latter has been described above, for the role-players in the coming ceremony, but in the other you have the opportunity to let the youngsters (Masonically at least) try their hands at taking the parts of the lodge Officers. In fact your lodge may have sufficient juniors to hold a Juniors' Night in lodge, although these days Past Masters' Nights generally seem to greatly outnumber the others. You can let some juniors look after the basic elements of the ceremony – the questions and answers of the Wardens and Deacons, and the Inner Guard and Tyler admitting the candidate. The working tools in all three degrees are useful solo exercises, as are the corner addresses in the first and second degrees, the questions and answers from the Master to the candidate (Deacon) and the charges in the second and third degrees. The obligations may be split into two, especially the longer first and third degree ones, and the first degree charge may be split into more. The traditional history and the second degree tracing board explanation can also be split into sections, and by the time you break down the first degree tracing board or some of the lectures you may have a half dozen or more taking part.

And then a thought comes into your mind – why not let the juniors deliver that first degree tracing board as a team, not just in the practice, but in the lodge as well? If your lodge is blessed with numerous juniors, they will each be several years from the Master's chair, so why not give them something to get their teeth into? If they are a good team, as happened in one of the Preston lodges after the Second World War when they received invitations from other lodges to demonstrate their capabilities, you then have juniors acting as ambassadors of your lodge. Even if you cannot aspire to those levels, the short sections of learning that each junior does will be usefully stored away for future reference when his turn comes to go through the Officers' progression to the Master's chair.

All of this organisation takes some planning, and time is something that a Director of Ceremonies requires in no small measure. However, the benefits can be enormous, because now you can see which of the juniors is inspired enough to learn, not just his section, but the next part in the sequence. In my early lodge years

I was allocated part of the first degree charge to learn, and surprising myself that it had not turned out to be too onerous, I learned the next paragraph, and then the next, and relatively soon I had the gist of the whole charge. However, I had never openly tackled more than a couple of sections in the junior practices and had only delivered the second degree working tools formally in lodge, when out of the blue the new Master asked me to deliver the charge to the first initiate in his year. Somebody had been quietly watching my enthusiasm and progress and decided that I could be entrusted with that responsibility, and I have no doubt the Director of Ceremonies and his predecessor at the practices had kept their eyes open for someone willing to put in the required amount of work. And you can benefit similarly, by observing which juniors are keen to learn and can undertake certain roles if required. It might be that one Officer informs you in good time that he cannot attend the next lodge meeting, and to have some eager and well-rehearsed junior understudies makes your life a lot easier in such a situation.

You are also able to spot the otherwise enthusiastic members who do not find learning easy, because not everyone is a born ritualist and we all learn at different rates. In their cases they may benefit from some additional tuition, perhaps for a few minutes after the lodge practice, or perhaps in their home if they wish it to be less formal. You will have to decide with your ADC how to split up this additional work, and you may also reassess the sizes of the chunks of ritual into which you split the ceremonies; you may perhaps select slightly smaller passages for some to cope with while others can be stretched into tackling longer ones. This is returning to man management, and tailoring the tasks to the capabilities of the different people, so no more needs to be repeated here.

Each of us has his own way of tackling a new item to learn, and the learning of the text is done in private, but you as Director of Ceremonies will be able to advise on different methods if asked, and one such method was outlined in the book for Principal Officers. As a final note, always place the emphasis on encouragement for anyone trying to learn a part of the ritual, rather than offering nit-picking and potentially destructive criticism. When the person is trying to deliver his part from memory, perhaps ask for his ritual book; then while he is performing you can mark in pencil where he missed words or put in the wrong ones, and perhaps where he paused or needed a prompt, so that he knows where to concentrate his revision. If the delivery was almost perfect, quietly congratulate him and inform him that he is very nearly there, but if he could make these few changes he would be spot on; the learning was done in private, and perhaps this encouragement should be made individually. And if you have a reputation in the lodge for being a good ritualist, this will be accepted as praise indeed, and will hopefully spur him on to greater things.

Lodges of Instruction

Some lodges have created a Lodge of Instruction. This is a practice organised under another name, but it is run on much more formal lines. The leader is designated the Preceptor, who is often the Director of Ceremonies of the lodge, and it requires formal minutes to be taken and a list of appointed Officers to be kept (BoC132-135). It is probable that there will be a schedule of tasks that each member is to undertake in turn, and a record kept of all of the items that he has mastered during his time in the Lodge of Instruction. The whole concept is to develop each Mason so that when he arrives at any rung on the progression of offices towards the Master's chair, he has a thorough grounding in everything he requires in order to do it well. It also spreads out the learning required by the Master for his year of office, because in strict Emulation lodges the Master conducts the whole of each ceremony from start to finish. This is in contrast to other lodges, which in their third degree ceremonies split the work between the Master and the IPM, with the latter delivering the traditional history. Of course, Masters of Emulation lodges have the chance of going to London to demonstrate a degree ceremony after which, if successfully completed, they are presented with a silver matchbox as a mark of their proven ability – the margins for error are very small, and the award is well merited.

Not every lodge requires a Lodge of Instruction, many preferring the more informal way of operating. But for the keen Masons who want to try this more formal type of practice, they will normally be welcome as visitors and will sometimes be allowed to join in, so you may want to ascertain where there are Lodges of Instruction in your area and on what nights they meet. In fact, it will do you no harm to visit yourself because, just as when visiting other lodges you can pick up tips on ways of interpreting the ritual, these formal sessions can provide a useful extension to your experience and, as you probably prefer to see any ritual performed well, you will enjoy watching some enthusiastic youngsters being put through their paces.

The Lodge Ritual

Although this section deals with man management, part of this is concerned with ensuring that each Officer and member understands the lodge ritual. If you are a strict Emulation lodge, then you are fortunate that this is the most common format to be published in books. However, the Nigerian ritual for example is also not far removed from that of Emulation, and lodges using other rituals closely related to Emulation are able to cope by using a standard book plus additional notes. However, in these days of computers and desktop publishing, it is more common for lodges to print their own version of the ritual for their members. Some lodges formally present a master copy of their ritual to a new Director of Ceremonies at his investiture, so that he is fully aware of the nuances that might have escaped his notice while an ordinary member. This copy may include additional notes by previous Directors of Ceremonies, to further explain various aspects of the ritual in detail.

From time to time the lodge may want to update its ritual. Occasionally Grand Lodge issues edicts about compulsory changes to the wording of the ritual, for example in the 1980s the penalties in the obligations were changed to emphasise their symbolic nature. As Director of Ceremonies you will probably head a small committee of members to discuss and draft revised sections of the current ritual, and a similar exercise will be necessary if you are starting a new lodge and agreeing the ritual to be followed. This committee will probably include the Secretary for any editorial input, although these days you may also have other members with considerable computer, information technology or publishing knowledge, and whose experience you can profitably call upon. It is a worthwhile intellectual exercise, as you may be assessing some aspects of the ceremonial in detail for the first time – items that you have never given a second thought to, but on which another member of the committee may have a different viewpoint – and suddenly the discussion broadens into the historical and other aspects of the lodge and Masonic ritual, and becomes very wide-ranging. It is also an interesting balance, to retain the traditional features of your ritual, while framing it for a lodge that is to operate in the 21st Century.

Perhaps if you are revising existing ritual, you will report back to the lodge to obtain general acceptance of what the committee has drafted, and then you or the Secretary will obtain quotations for printing books of the final approved text and distribute copies to the members. If you are a new lodge, you may let the ritual settle down by utilising the draft version for the first few years, finalise any corrections you have made as the ceremonies have been performed, and then go to print.

Members Losing Enthusiasm

In the course of running many of the practices, perhaps sharing the work with your ADC, you will sometimes notice members who begin to attend infrequently. Perhaps they are very busy at work, which may take them away from home for extensive parts of the week, or they may have young children to cope with, but you will notice when they start to miss practices without any prior apology. This could be one of the first signs that they are less enthusiastic about the lodge and its ritual than others, and if they fall out of the routine of attending the lodge and practice meetings, it may not be too long before their resignation follows.

The Secretary is able to check lodge attendances from the attendance register, and you and he need to liaise if there is a potential problem developing. The initiate is the star of his first evening, and he is the central focus of his passing and raising ceremonies, but in the larger lodges the wait before he starts on the ladder of lodge offices leading to the Chair may be prolonged. This may be the time to check if he would like to enjoy a fuller role in lodge proceedings, and also to assess if the ceremonies could be broken into smaller parts in order to let some of the juniors participate. Some Provinces recommend that Past Masters perform all of the ceremonial work in the lodge, as a way of keeping them involved after their year in the Chair, but this is less than helpful in encouraging the youngsters to do anything significant.

This may also be the time for you, his proposer or his seconder to talk over with him the progression of offices leading to the Master's chair, and to point out that people develop at their own rate by learning small parts of the ritual before tackling the bigger chunks. If you have a lot of enthusiastic youngsters, then why not have a Juniors' Night in the lodge, and see how they perform – I would wager they will not let themselves or the lodge down, and just watch the renewed interest in attending the practice meetings. If work or family commitments require his attention for some time to come, then ensure he understands that he is welcome at the lodge whenever he is able to attend, and that when the pressures diminish and he is ready to start to participate more actively in the life of the lodge, it will always be ready to assist him in any way it can. We are all members of the Masonic family, and the positive support that a lodge can give any of its members, and not just when they are ill, should never be underestimated or forgotten.

In a similar vein, watch for the Past Masters losing interest in the lodge after they have been IPM and Tyler, if the latter office follows the IPM. They were in the top echelons of the lodge for several years, with pedestals and reserved seats at the meals, etc., and suddenly they are not having much to do. You as Director of Ceremonies should ensure that everyone is busy, and if you have several candidates then you might suggest to the Master that each lodge Officer could do one of each of the Craft ceremonies, and then perhaps let someone else take over his role in any repeat ceremonies. If traditionally you have Juniors' and Past Masters' Nights, then all of the Officers are aware that in some meetings each year they will be replaced, and there will be no potential resentment. If you do not have such traditions, then you might suggest to the Lodge Committee that a very slight change of direction in organising and carrying out the ceremonies may be in the best interests of the lodge and its members; most members will go along with the suggestion to try it to see what reaction is produced. For example, in my lodge an Installing Master was expected to present all of the working tools in full to his successor. One Master approaching the installation hand-over had never delivered the third degree working tools, and I was asked to assist him by delivering them on his behalf (my first time too). Two other juniors asked if they could deliver the second and first degree working tools, and the Past Masters went into a huddle with the Master, who declared that he would in no way be insulted if the lodge removed all of the tool presentations from him on this occasion. Such were the plaudits for the three juniors and congratulations on the obvious good health of the lodge, from the representative of the Provincial Grand Master to everyone else who was allowed to speak in lodge and at the banquet, that a new lodge tradition was instantly born! Try to take a problem, and turn it into an opportunity for the lodge to benefit from.

General Ceremonial

Preparing the Lodge Room

As Director of Ceremonies you will need to arrive early for the lodge meeting in order to check that all is ready for the evening. You may in fact be responsible for preparing the lodge room, or you may have someone else who does that for you – such as the Tyler – but in your particular role you are responsible for everything that happens on the day. As an *aide mémoire* a checklist of various items to remember is given in the Appendix, but you may find that your lodge has additional items that are required in the different ceremonies, so treat the list as a basis rather than a catch-all.

As well as checking that you are ready for the meeting, try to spot each Officer in turn as he arrives so that you ensure your whole team is present, because you may be approaching a Past Master or two to fill in for any unforeseen absentees. If it is the first lodge meeting after the installation, then there may be several promoted Officers checking their new bearings, so try to have some time for each of them if required. And if you have substitutes for some Officers who have warned you they will not be there, welcome them as well – especially any juniors you have asked to be in the team temporarily. They will be nervous and may want a few words or a quick revision of some aspects of their duties in order to calm their nerves. If you have a Juniors' Night, then there may be several butterflies in stomachs, and you and/or the ADC should be there as a totem for them to gather round and gain mutual support. Remind all participants to look to you if they need a prompt or guidance where to go next, and try to smile – it has a wonderfully calming and reassuring effect, because if you look tense and worried, it can be contagious.

The other people you should look out for are the Master and the Secretary. Both may have breaking news that additional items will be necessary – the Master may have picked up items of importance during his travels around other lodges since the last meeting, while the Secretary may have some recent correspondence from Grand or Provincial Grand Lodge that has to be acted upon. If there has been a very recent death in the lodge, or of a senior Officer in Grand Lodge or the Province, then the lodge may be asked to stand as a mark of respect for departed merit, a few words may be read in honour of his passing, and some Officers may be wearing black rosettes. Hopefully the grapevine has worked before the meeting, with the Master or Secretary having already warned you, but always expect the unexpected.

There may be some visitors wanting to see you. If you have any dignitaries attending, then they will probably make themselves known to you, so that you can inform them of the lodge's method of operating and they can check any other details that they need to know. You may also have some members introducing their guests and confirming that they can vouch to having sat with them in open lodge previously. They will certainly introduce any guests who are Entered Apprentices or Fellowcrafts, because they probably require one of the lodge aprons to wear. Also there may be some newcomers as guests who have not been before and do not know any member, and they should produce their Grand Lodge Certificates and letters of good standing from their own lodges, and then they need proving. This you may do, or delegate it to your ADC or the Junior Warden, and you may want to remind them that the visitor only needs to be proved in the highest degree that the lodge will be operating in during the meeting. The ADC or Junior Warden should report back to you that all is well, as you are on behalf of the Master the ultimate guardian that all Masonic protocol has been followed on a lodge night.

Opening Business of the Lodge

Your first duty may be to form an incoming procession for the Master, and this may include not only his Officers but also the lodge and visiting Past Masters and Masters of other lodges. Newcomers may need a quick word on the format, which can be perhaps to follow the Deacons, and stop when they stop and turn inwards to form a guard of honour for the Master as he makes his way to the pedestal. Then if the visitors peel away from the procession while the Wardens are placed in position, advise the visiting brethren where they should sit – perhaps Provincial Officers in the North East and Masters in the South East, etc., as your lodge tradition requires.

You then hope the previous nights of practice stand all of the Officers in good stead, as they go through the formalities of opening. If it starts well, it usually continues in the same vein; if it starts otherwise, then hope that at some time one Officer manages to speak correctly and confidently, and that the confidence spreads. Nod encouragement to the Deacons if they look to see when they should be opening the lodge furniture such as the tracing board, and also to the IPM if he opens the Bible. Then enjoy the opening ode if you sing one and have not done so earlier, and sit down; some lodges follow the Master in sitting, while in others either the Master or you invite everyone to be seated.

Now you can let the Master go through the agenda items in turn. The Secretary may read the summons convening the meeting, a member may read an ancient charge, and then the minutes of the previous meeting may be read and put to the vote, either directly by the Master or after a formal proposition and seconding by two members, perhaps the Wardens. The Deacons or Secretary will carry the Minute Book for signing by the Master and possibly by the Wardens. The Secretary or Assistant Secretary may then summarise or read the minutes of the previous Lodge Committee meeting. The Treasurer may need permission to pay some accounts, and this may again need a formal proposition and seconding for acceptance, as required by the lodge bylaws. But all of these items are routine, and you will have run through them at several practices before, especially with a new Master and Officers after their installation and investiture, so there should be no surprises here.

You as Director of Ceremonies may have to enquire about the numbers staying to dine, if the meal is pre-booked or otherwise as there may be extras, and you will probably ask who is not staying for the festive board after checking that everyone has signed the attendance register. You or the Inner Guard may then inform the Tyler to tell the caterer that meals are required for the number in the Tyler's book, minus those who cannot stay, plus those who did not sign in, plus the initiate if there is one, as he will not have signed the book. A little mental agility will be required of you, but hopefully it is not too onerous.

Visitors, Processions and Salutes

Most visitors in the lodge room when the meeting began will have been briefed by their hosts as to the protocol in the lodge. However, some visitors may have arrived before their hosts, and do not seem to be totally *au fait* with the Hall layout and the organisation of the lodge. They may introduce themselves to you or the Secretary, but it would be useful if the lodge team looking after visitors – the Junior Warden and his Stewards (remember the installation addresses?) – could be charged to keep a look-out for such newcomers and welcome them and introduce them to the Master, etc. If you have someone from another Constitution, then he may have brought a letter of introduction from his Grand Lodge and/or United Grand Lodge. He will still need to prove himself and to produce confirmation of good standing within his lodge. The Secretary may read out that letter as soon as the lodge is opened, and you will of course escort the visitor to be formally greeted and welcomed by the Master on behalf of the lodge. You may have some visitors or even members who turn up late, and after due announcement of their names via the Inner Guard and Junior Warden, perhaps you, the ADC or one of the Deacons will escort them into the lodge room to formally greet the Master and apologise for being late. They will then be escorted to a suitable seat in the lodge room, which may vary depending on their ranks, e.g. Provincial Officers in the North East, etc.

It may be that the visitor who is late is well known in the lodge, but you should perhaps enquire which member can vouch for him. Some lodges organise their meetings to conduct their essential opening business and then formally introduce visitors, and they often request the vouching member to stand and confirm so individually. If the visitor is not known or vouched for, then he will have to be proved – by you, the ADC or the Junior Warden. If the lodge has a Past Master who is acting as Tyler, I cannot see why he should not prove any latecomer appropriately – and if it is an installation, a Junior Warden who is a Master Mason cannot prove an Installed Master in any case. The Tyler can then report through the Inner Guard that there is a visiting latecomer and he has already been proved. However, the occurrence is fairly rare, and the Junior Warden when being invested is informed that he has a special responsibility for the examination of visitors, so often it is he who will leave the lodge and return with confirmation that the visitor may be admitted. This has been done to me on a few occasions when I have been late and a first-time visitor, and as a suggestion it might be a nice touch for whoever proves the visitor to personally accompany him into the lodge room to introduce him and confirm that he has been proved, and then let him greet the Master.

If there is a special visitor, perhaps representing the Provincial Grand Master at the installation meeting, it would be a courtesy for him to be met on his arrival at the Hall and introduced to the Master, Secretary and candidate or Master Elect as appropriate. It is also probable that he will merit a special entrance into the lodge after it has opened. Some Provinces insist that the lodge should have opened into the third degree for such a reception, but others allow an entrance in the first degree so that the visitor can see the opening ceremonies in the other degrees. If the visitor is very senior, he will be accompanied by the Provincial Director of Ceremonies or one of his Deputies, and you will leave everything to him. If, however, you need to organise the reception, you will probably leave the lodge room and then re-enter to announce the visitor and other senior guests in the accompanying procession. This is a time when the Secretary needs to have forewarned you who is coming so that you have an idea of the list of titles you will have to reel off. If your memory is not as sharp as it used to be, there is no crime in having a crib sheet to read from – it is more important to make the correct pronouncements rather than a near miss. If the Deacons did not accompany you out of the lodge, you will request them to join you at the door of the lodge room, and you will lead the procession to the East. Probably the Deacons will follow you, spaced slightly apart, so that when they and the rest of the procession turn inwards, they will form a guard of honour for the principal visitor to walk through in order to greet the Master.

Once the visitors are seated, you may conduct the salutations to those whom your lodge regularly salutes; some lodges perform these towards the end of the meeting, near to or in the risings, although as a form of welcome it seems a little late, but each lodge has its own traditions. Remember that salutes are silent, and greetings are noisy. All salutes begin with a step, as do all grips except the pass grip, while the sign of reverence has neither a step nor is it cut afterwards. One routine you may adopt is to stand, give the recipient of the salutes a court bow, request the brethren below that rank to stand, call upon them to give a number of salutes of the degree in which the lodge is opened, ask them to make a half-turn to the East and to order, lead the salutes, request the brethren to be seated, another court bow to the recipient, and return to your seat.

The salutations will normally begin with the Grand Officers, including the Provincial Grand Master, his Deputy and Assistants (in the Metropolitan Grand Lodge this may extend to Group Chairman, as it does not have Assistant Provincial Grand Masters), and these will be saluted before the others. You may also have VW Grand Ranks as well, perhaps the Provincial Chaplain who has an acting or past Grand Chaplain appellation, and these will also precede the remaining Grand Officers. The salutes are different for the different ranks, and the MW Grand Master and Pro Grand Master receive 11, the RW Deputy and Assistant Grand Master receive nine, and other RW brethren are saluted seven and VW brethren five times in any Province. The Deputy and Assistant Provincial Grand Masters are saluted five times in their own Provinces, and other Grand Officers merit three.

With regard to the Provincial Grand Officers you also have an additional hierarchy of ranks, from the Provincial Senior Grand Warden down, and you will mention any visiting Provincial Wardens that are present or the senior Past Provincial Officer present, and certainly the representative of the Provincial Grand Master, and without having Grand Rank they all merit three salutations. It may be your lodge custom to name any other acting ranks that are visiting, and immediately after the new Provincial honours or promotions are conferred your lodge may like to formally congratulate those members who have been honoured in this way. The order of the Provincial ranking is included in the Appendix, and if there are a lot of people to name as Grand and Provincial Grand Officers, then you may agree to share the workload with your ADC, one conducting the salutations to one set, and the other to the other.

Before the closing business of the lodge, the dignitaries may exercise their prerogative to retire from the lodge early. This usefully deals with some of the bar traffic before the bulk of the attendees arrive, and it will normally be the reverse of the equivalent incoming procession. One point to bear in mind, and the Provincial workshops will certainly have alluded to this, is that in many Provinces it is protocol for the representative or the most senior member of the Grand or

Provincial Grand Officers to be conducted to his place at the head of the procession only after everyone else is in place. Some Provinces prefer you to take the hand of the Grand Officer for example and guide him into his place, others prefer you lead in front of him, so check Provincial protocol. If the person being escorted is elderly, he may appreciate a hand to lean on, but you can have discussed this with him before the meeting began. The Deacons may cross their wands for the dignitaries to exit underneath, and when they have all gone, you and the Deacons return to your places, and everyone relaxes.

Other Items of Business

If there is to be no ceremony worked or demonstrated, it is probable that a lecture may be delivered, and you will obviously have been introduced to the speaker. Each will have his own preferences for delivering his talk, some wanting to use a lectern if available, others wishing to move around the lodge room, perhaps pointing out various features during their presentation. You will need someone to put the lectern in place if required (ADCs have their uses at times), and you yourself will accompany the speaker to the position from where he will begin his talk. If he is using electronic aids, such as projectors or computer images, then the appropriate equipment will have been prepared ready for placing on the lodge room floor, but such special aids will probably have been set up by the speaker himself beforehand. After his talk and perhaps some questions, he will need escorting back to his seat, and possibly the Master, or you, or some other brother will have a short speech of thanks to deliver, but between you and the Secretary you should be aware of some of the content of the lecture, and such a speech can have been partly rehearsed at least in draft before the meeting. You should note that the content of some lectures requires the lodge to be called off and on again, and this is performed mainly by the Junior Warden; ensure he is aware of these short extra pieces of ritual.

With candidates for initiation, joining members and the conferring of honorary membership, there is a ball ballot. The ballots can be taken all together, but if the allowed number of black or nay balls is exceeded, then the ballots need to be repeated as individual ones (you may deem it preferable to combine honorary and joining membership ballots, but leave candidates for initiation separate). The bylaws will indicate how many black balls are allowed whilst still not rejecting the candidate, and while Grand Lodge allows up to two black balls before there is an unsuccessful ballot, some lodges reduce that number to one or even none. The Deacons can either distribute a black and a white ball to each member (using the one-drawer ballot box; the two-drawer aye/nay box requires only one ball), or remain at the Secretary's table to hand them out (whichever your lodge prefers). If it is the first time they have performed this task, they may be looking at you for confirmation that they are doing it correctly. The Deacons must give out the balls to members, otherwise by mistake or deliberately a member may take more than one ball and the ballot may be adversely affected. The ballot box must be shown to the Master prior to the ballot, to confirm there are no lingering balls from previous ballots, and you or the Deacons may do this. The members vote in turn, and the ballot box is taken to the Master, perhaps by you, to ascertain the outcome, which the Master declares, and the Wardens will confirm the result in turn if that is your lodge custom, but the ballot box drawer should not be displayed. Afterwards the unused balls are collected, and this needs to be secret as well, so the balls are returned into the same or another box or into a bag.

In the annual business meeting, or the meeting preceding the installation, there will be the ballots for the Master Elect, the Treasurer, and the Tyler if required (if the last-named is a member of the lodge, he can be appointed with the other Officers). Because of the range of members who are eligible for the offices – and the Master Elect for example can be a time-served Warden, a Past Master of yours or any other lodge, or even the Master of another lodge (by dispensation) – paper ballots are used for the Master Elect and Treasurer. The Deacons will normally hand out the slips for the ballots, and you may allow them to remove their gloves if this makes the handling of the paper more efficient. They collect the completed slips for the Master to scrutinise, perhaps reading out loud the names on the first returns, although strictly only the result needs to be announced, and the lucky winner normally stands to acknowledge his good fortune. The Tyler's election, if he is not appointed, only requires a show of hands, as with the confirmation of the minutes.

Other people may be elected at the business or other meeting, such as auditors, Group and Masonic Hall representatives, and each will need to be formally proposed and seconded. Normally the Secretary earmarks several members to perform these actions, and the votes are by a show of hands. Each of the elected members may respond to thank the brethren for their new-found or continued confidence in their capabilities. It may be usual to then receive the Almoner's report, the Charity or Festival representative's report, and reports from other appointees as required.

Closing Down the Meeting
The Master then initiates the final part of the meeting by asking if there is any other business to be transacted within the lodge, and this may include propositions and notices of motion; the former perhaps referring to potential new lodge members, and the latter possibly to the Treasurer wanting to raise the subscriptions again. He then enquires if there is any correspondence from Grand Lodge, Provincial Grand Lodge, or from anyone else, a sequence which is informally known in many lodges

as "the risings", because he and perhaps the Wardens may rise in turn to announce each enquiry.

The Secretary will summarise each set of correspondence, and after the first two the Grand Officers and the Provincial Grand Officers may respectively bring greetings and perhaps congratulations on how the meeting has gone. They may also choose to retire early, and you will organise the formal processions as discussed before. On the third rising all visitors may bring greetings, or you may – at an installation for example – limit the reply to one. It is a shame if you do impose a limit, because each visitor is an ambassador of his lodge and maybe of a different Province or Constitution, and a few words from each lodge represented takes only a little extra time. If you encourage each visiting lodge to respond briefly, and you can emphasise the brevity, then it may be better that you walk around the lodge room in a clockwise direction to stand opposite each brother speaking, so all are confident that by catching your eye their turn will come.

The Senior Warden may then request the lodge members to stand and bring their own greetings to their Master, who after thanking all of the speakers will gavel to begin closing the lodge. The interchanges are shorter than in the opening, and after the IPM has closed the Bible and returned to his place, you will begin forming the retiring procession, perhaps while the closing hymn is being sung. This may be done by you or the ADC walking round the lodge and picking up the Deacons and Wardens in turn, or you may have rehearsed it so that they form the procession on their own.

You will then bring in the Master and any dignitaries left behind, perhaps a Grand Officer in your own lodge, and acting Provincial Officers not requested to be in the guard of honour for the previous retiring processions. In some lodges, if Past Provincial ranks are also invited, then the lodge room would be almost empty, which is not particularly desirable. Your lodge may also invite the Masters of other lodges to join the final procession, and it is a courtesy that is always well received; they are after all the titular heads of their lodges, and it should always be a pleasure to receive them into your lodge as visitors. You then request the procession to leave, followed by other visitors, possibly in order of seniority if you wish, and then lodge members. And your lodge room work is over, only the meal to cope with now.

Special Meetings

There are many special meetings that lodges can enjoy, for example the consecration of a new lodge. They can also include banner dedications, members' personal celebrations – 50th, 60th, etc. – or the lodge's similar anniversaries, and these can go beyond the typical lifetimes of members to 100th, 150th, 200th and even 250th celebrations. For the lodge Director of Ceremonies these are absolutely brilliant, because Province will send the Provincial Director of Ceremonies, or Grand Lodge will send its equivalent for the most important anniversaries, and they have all of the running order to sort out. You of course can volunteer to assist, but the burden of responsibility has shifted from your shoulders, so you can enjoy the meeting along with the rest of your members and possibly watch a master craftsman directing the ceremonial.

The Craft Ceremonies

Preparation

Of course, the above section has skirted round the main events of most lodge meetings, the ceremonies in the three degrees. This is where the lodge team of Officers combine to reproduce their perfect ceremony as at the prior practice meeting and, if they do so, you can relax. If it does not go perfectly, there is plenty for you to do. It is not perhaps surprising that when a ceremony starts off being less than perfect, it can go steadily downhill thereafter. You need to be vigilant, to check if any Officer is glancing at you for last-minute corrective advice where he is going or for a prompt, and your brain will be going through every word and action in the ceremony in order to assist instantly if called upon. This is no easy task, as most Directors of Ceremonies will testify, and you should share the load where possible with your ADC, perhaps splitting up sections of the ceremony, or one of you following the Assistant Officers and especially the Deacons, and the other looking after the Principal Officers. Make sure that your back-up prompter is not falling asleep during the ceremony, which may start very well and lull everyone into a false sense of security, only for a prompt to be required and not be instantly forthcoming.

The Officers should be confident about where the action is to take place and the sequence of events, as hopefully all will have attended the prior practice. If any have missed that meeting, then you should have a quick word with them immediately before the lodge meeting, or even previously by telephone after they missed the practice, so that they are able to perform to their best abilities. If they go slightly wrong, then hopefully a few hand signals or quiet words of advice will correct events before they go too far from the desired format.

The Three Degree Ceremonies

So without going into minute detail over every ceremony, much of which has been covered in the books for the Assistant and Principal Officers, what are the key aspects in each? In the second and third degrees, the candidate has his test questions to answer, and the Deacon should be able to help him answer if he needs assistance. After he is entrusted and has retired, the lodge is opened in the higher degree, and any floor preparations made, possibly by the Deacons; ensure that they lay out the various items as you want, and no-one minds a few whispered instructions at this stage, or even the Deacons approaching you for additional advice. You may note that there is no need to hide the lower degree tracing boards when opening into the second and third respectively; as the Master normally states when closing down, work is resumed – not restarted – in the lower degrees.

Before the candidate enters, check that you hear the appropriate password from him while being questioned by the Inner Guard. When he steps into the room, quickly check that the Tyler has prepared him properly, and if not you may have to go across to make the necessary adjustments – and you will have to do so rapidly in the third because of the reduced visibility away from the door. The circuits of the lodge should be accomplished without any problem, but watch in case the Deacon fails to halt before the final circuit. Then the candidate will approach the East in due form and with the appropriate number of steps and, unless this enactment is completely haywire, leave it uncorrected – to make the candidate repeat it properly will be lost on him, as he does not yet know there is a different method; the visitors will put whatever they have seen down to the idiosyncrasies of your lodge, and you can kill the Deacon later.

The Master should cope with the obligation and the short sections before and after, with the Immediate Past Master or you or the back-up prompter helping where needed. The Master or others will go through the next stages of the ceremonies – the signs and penalties in the first two, the circuit round the Wardens and the investiture of the new apron, and the moralisation on the working tools before leaving the room. Your main role will be waiting to assist with any prompts. There is a longer build-up in the third, with the Wardens taking over from the Deacons, and any oddities in how they do so are thankfully difficult to spot. You will have to rely on the three Principal Officers helping each other if needed – they are after all close to each other; then the candidate receives his introduction to the penalties and signs before retiring.

All of the ceremonies follow on with additional explanations on what has been enacted so far, the third including the working tools. You may have the explanations of the tracing boards and the charges included in this section, so there is not a great deal of movement around the lodge room, but there are a lot of words for you to follow should any brother require your assistance. On the other hand, in these sections it is often the more capable ritualists who are called into play, and hopefully you will have little to do.

The Installation Ceremony
The installation is different, because there are the open parts of the ceremony and

the inner workings. Life becomes much more fun for you, because the Installing Wardens may be different from the regular lodge Officers, and your lodge may have a tradition of inviting Masters or senior brethren of other lodges to fill these positions. Hopefully they will have attended your installations before and will have an idea of what is expected of them, and they will obviously be invited to your practice meetings so that they can run through what they have to do. You may already think that it is difficult enough for your own lodge Officers to follow your lodge traditions, but now you will have to possibly persuade people inured in their own lodge traditions to temporarily adopt yours for one meeting. Hopefully they are willing volunteers, and so will put in the requisite work.

The installation meeting also involves the participation of many other lodge members, to present the Master Elect, to address the new Principal Officers, the brethren and all of the Officers as required, and presenting the working tools in the various parts of the ceremony. Usefully they are all stand-alone pieces that can be learned in isolation by the respective people and, as long as they know where to deliver the items from, they may not necessarily want to go through the passages in a practice meeting. You might encourage all the juniors who are participating to demonstrate their capabilities in the practice meeting, because for them it will be a relatively new experience performing parts of the ritual in the lodge room and in front of probably many more attendees than at other meetings. Some lodges expect the new Master to address all of his Officers in full, so the Master Elect may well want to rehearse all of the addresses in front of an audience for his own peace of mind.

For the installation, as with most special lodge occasions, your members may be in dinner suits or formal morning attire and all Provincial and Grand Officers should wear full dress regalia. Because the installation is such a different ceremony, you cannot relax as you may have been able to do at previous lodge meetings. You and the Secretary will probably arrive earlier than normal to ensure everything is laid out properly, including reserved seats in the lodge room and place cards on the meal tables. You will also have a list of people performing different aspects of the ceremony, and you will want to check each of them as they arrive, otherwise you will rapidly need to identify some willing volunteers to fill in for them. You will certainly have a senior member of the Province coming as the representative of the Provincial Grand Master, and he may be attended by the Provincial Deacons and the Director of Ceremonies or one of his Deputies. With such an entourage, much of the processing and saluting duties are lifted off your shoulders, which is always welcome.

After the entrance of the dignitaries, it may be your lodge custom for the Officers to line up and hand in their collars of office to the Master, which not only lets him thank them personally, but he can pass the collars to you or the ADC to place on a hanger ready for investing the new Officers. I never cease to be surprised how many lodges that request their Officers to line up in this manner, juniors first or last, manage to muddle through the seniority issue, which is probably stated every month on their summons as a reminder. However, an alert IPM can make adjustments in the order as the collars are being handed to him so that they are ready for distribution to the new Officers, or perhaps during the pause before inviting juniors back into the lodge room you can rearrange them. You may then need to escort all of the Installing Officers to their respective places in the lodge room. The Master Elect is presented, possibly by you or another senior member of the lodge, and obligated in the second degree, with most of the work being done by the Master – and also the Master Elect if he has been asked to learn his first obligation. The lodge then opens in the third degree, and the remaining juniors leave the lodge room. There may be an entrusting if your lodge uses extended inner working, then the Board of Installed Masters is opened and the inner working conducted, led by the Installing Master, but possibly assisted by other Installed Masters.

The juniors then return sequentially in the three degrees, and you or the Installing Master ask them to salute the new Master in passing, and then to greet him with three or five salutes as appropriate. It is very useful to rehearse this with the juniors at the practice meetings, and perhaps if they do not always attend the practices you can go through the sequence after the previous lodge meeting, or even arrange to meet them early before the installation starts. It does not look professional to have to tutor them in the actual ceremony, and yet many lodges seem to do so – which implies their juniors are not properly educated. You will restrict the returning juniors to Master Masons, Fellowcrafts and Entered Apprentices in the separate degrees, or split what may be a large number of Master Masons more evenly into three sets of juniors re-entering the lodge. You may also hand the working tools of each degree to those presenting them to the Master and, if these are juniors, a reassuring smile or wink may not go amiss in calming their nerves.

The Master then appoints and invests his Officers for the year. As Director of Ceremonies you may immediately begin your escorting duties, or you may leave the first few to the Installing Master until you are appointed. When you are on escort duty, you and the ADC should be able to co-operate efficiently to collect the various members and their emblems of office, present the new Officers to the Master to be invested, and then escort them to their places around the lodge room. You may agree that you will collect the people and the ADC the objects, or you take it in turns to look after each Officer to and from the Master. If you have an honorary organist, he cannot wear that collar of office, but it would be a nice touch after the Tyler's investiture for the Master to formally thank him for past and future services, perhaps by you escorting him to and from the East. Then follow the addresses to the Master, Wardens and brethren; each person delivering an address may require escorting to and from a suitable place in the lodge room. Some lodges invite the representative to take part in the ceremony, and will often suggest he might deliver the address to the brethren, so that particular escorting duty needs to be done formally. Hopefully you know this address well because, standing close behind him, you will be in the perfect position to prompt the representative quietly if and when required.

After the investiture of a Past Master's jewel to the Immediate Past Master and perhaps a congratulatory speech from the representative, the lodge reverts to its normal business mode, which has already been covered previously so, apart from the probable early retirement of the representative and dignitaries, you should see a familiar sequence of events as in ordinary lodge meetings. If there is a cheque to give to the representative, it would probably be most neatly fitted into the few words that the Master says in answer to the representative's comments. After the close of the meeting, there is the banquet to oversee, which makes the installation meeting a marathon for any Director of Ceremonies.

If the Master Elect is unable to attend on the normal installation date, the lodge will try to obtain a dispensation to move to a date when he can be there. If he still cannot attend, and there is no time to ballot for another Master Elect, then the current Master must continue in office for a second year, or even a third year by dispensation. In these circumstances the lodge may conduct the shortened installation ceremony for him to reassume the Chair, or you may simply proclaim him to continue as Master and salute him accordingly, and he will then invest his new Officers. If, however, the Master is going to stay on for a second year, and he cannot as Master Elect attend the installation, then you can proclaim that he is continuing in office for the ensuing year, and another Installed Master will invest the new lodge Officers in his stead. This will be a very short installation meeting, because the proclamation can be made in the first degree, so there are no obligations, no second or third degree opening and closing or tools (no-one to present them to), etc. If these circumstances have never previously arisen in your lodge, you may request the Secretary to seek guidance from the Provincial office on its preferred form of ceremony or proclamation.

Out of Lodge Functions

Installation and General Lodge Meals

At festive boards, meals and social functions, you as Director of Ceremonies are kept busy for the whole time, as organiser and toastmaster. Some lodges first request the presence of the new Master in the Provincial assembly room, so those Officers can formally toast his good health for the coming year, and you will have to see that he excuses himself from other people to be there punctually. At an installation or a major meeting, the representative may also request to meet the brethren of the lodge less formally, and you will accompany him in order to introduce the different members to him, both the juniors and the seniors. In bygone days many representatives and senior Provincial Officers were very aloof and tended to mix only with their peers; these days there is a greater intermixing of Masonic status, and the Craft is the better for it. You may start the formal proceedings by announcing that the Master is about to enter the dining room, perhaps with the senior distinguished guests, and you then lead him to his seat at the top table. It is a courtesy if those brethren whom you pass on the way to the top table do not have their backs to the Master, and depending on the geography of the dining room they may stand back from their chairs to let him pass between, or turn outwards as he passes them. You then call silence for the Chaplain to pronounce grace (if the Chaplain is in Holy Orders, you will ask him for a blessing), and afterwards ensure the Master is seated – the rest should follow his example, but if not then invite them to do so.

There may be wine-taking at the meals, especially the installation banquet, and a selection of toasts is given in the Appendix, although your lodge may have other wine-taking traditions that they enjoy. Some lodges will take wine after every course of the meal, while others will have them all after the first and possibly second course, to allow the remainder of the meal to be eaten in peace. You will announce each wine-taking after the Principal Officers have gavelled for attention, and draw the Master's chair back slightly to help him stand. It is usual for the representative to take wine with not only the Master, but also with the rest of the brethren, and you will offer him the same courtesy. You and the Treasurer will need to keep an eye on the wine on the tables if it is provided by the lodge, to ensure the Stewards keep an ample but not necessarily profuse supply for the brethren and particularly the guests to enjoy.

After the meal is over, and possibly the caterers have cleared away the plates, you will call on the Chaplain to return thanks, and then you start on the toast list, possibly after singing a verse of the National Anthem if you have not done so in lodge. Each Province will have a preferred list of toasts to be taken, and you and the Master simply follow this, an example of which is given in the Appendix. It will be helpful if you run through the pronunciation of the toast list before the installation day, to ensure the Master and Wardens manage to avoid the "Programme Master" and "Provisional Grand Master", etc., as any mistakes they may make are evidence of a lack of tuition from you. Sometimes the Master proposes all of the toasts before his own, while in other lodges the Wardens assist, perhaps one proposing toast three and the other toast five, and you will take the toast list to them and call on each in turn to propose them. The neatest way is for the Master to gavel when you are behind the person who is to propose the toast, you then call the brethren to attend to the next toast, and the proposer explains to whom the toast is directed; it is better to avoid numbering the toast in your announcement. Some lodges have traditional ways of responding to toasts – by applause, by one knock, or perhaps by firing. If the last, then the Master or you will need to lead the brethren, so be sure you remember how it is done.

There may be a reply to the toasts, by a Grand Officer or a Provincial Grand Officer, or they may both be answered in one reply to toast five. If the respondent is the representative, or even when a very distinguished guest is present at a meeting other than the installation, some Provinces request a short biography of that person is given by the Master or Director of Ceremonies. In this situation these people will fortunately have prepared such a *résumé*, and you merely read it all or just some highlights by agreement with them. You then help them to their feet (not insinuating that they are by this time incapable of standing unaided) by easing out the chair as they rise, and hope they find something nice to say about the lodge and its workings. And you can be assured that they will have seen almost everything, and that they will report back to Province on the state of the lodge if they have been requested to do so. You should remain standing behind the person, ready to assist him in reseating himself by easing in the chair again, and do not start pushing the chair prematurely against his knees as a sign he should perhaps consider finishing his speech, whatever you think of it.

If at the installation meeting the lodge defers the charity collection until the banquet, you may arrange for it to follow the toast to Provincial Officers. You will need to have organised the Charity Steward and Stewards to collect the alms as quickly as possible, and the Treasurer to count it so the total can be announced later in the evening if your lodge does so. The next toast is to the Master and may be given by the IPM or another brother – perhaps his proposer into Masonry – and you will need to introduce him, having warned the Master to keep an eye on you and gavel as soon as you have arrived behind the chair of that person. After he has finished, if it is an installation, there may be the Master's song delivered by members or visitors, and they probably will not need any introduction, as the accompanist will provide his own. Note in some lodges they do not allow smoking before this song out of consideration for the vocal chords of the singer(s), some do not allow smoking at all, and others give permission after the second toast of the evening.

It is not unusual for a first-time Master to become emotional on hearing the Master's song sung, perhaps by a long-standing friend or even a family member and, if the lodge allows people to leave their seats for a short time after the song to greet their friends individually, this will allow him time to recover. If everyone stays seated, you may pause for a short while before inviting him to respond for the same reason. After his speech he may finish by toasting the Installing Master and his team, or make a separate speech, and the IPM may or may not respond. If the representative has to leave early, he will normally wait until after the Master's speech, and you may lead him out of the room but obviously you cannot go with him to see him off the premises, so it is a good idea to delegate one or more of the senior lodge members to accompany him as a courtesy, and they can afterwards rejoin you in the dining room.

Then may follow the toast to Masonic charities, and if the total collected earlier is known, the Charity Steward or whoever proposes the toast can inform the assembly of the sum raised, otherwise the Master can do so in his closing remarks. The toast to absent brethren may come next, or if your tradition is to keep to a specific time it may have already been taken and, if there is a sung verse or two, you will need to check that the pianist is ready to accompany the singing. After this there may be a toast to the Founders at installations, and whoever has been assigned this task – some lodges ask juniors to do it – you will need to locate him and introduce him accordingly.

You have now arrived at the toast to the visitors, and this is probably to be proposed by the Junior Warden or ostensible steward of the lodge, although some lodges allow others to do it on occasions. You may remind the proposer that he should couple the name and lodge affiliation of the respondent before the glasses are raised, and you make your way to the person so named. This hopefully should not be the first time he has been informed that he is expected to reply, a service normally performed by you or the Secretary immediately after the lodge meeting, unless beforehand the Master has already invited someone to do it. There may be more than one response, especially at installations and other major occasions, and you will call for order before each one speaks. You or the Master (by gavelling) will call on the Tyler for his toast, to be given either from near to where he was sitting or perhaps from behind the Master, and then you may call on the Master for the few final words. NOW you can heave a sigh of relief and begin to enjoy yourself, because your duties for the evening are at last over.

Social Events and Ladies' Functions

Your lodge may hold special meals for the brethren, such as Olde English Nights and other occasions where the emphasis is on enjoyment of the entertainment and possibly raising money for charity, and the toast list may be adapted. There may be very short or even no responses to the toasts, but all of the first five should be honoured. Hopefully a band of lodge members will have sorted out the bulk of the activities for the evening, and you effectively hand over to them, probably returning to introduce the toast to the visitors and the Tyler's toast at the end of the festivities.

Those lodges which after a meeting dine with their ladies occasionally or frequently will already be aware that the toast list is very truncated compared with occasions when only brethren are present, and the same applies to lodge socials and Ladies' Evenings. As Director of Ceremonies you primarily still attend on the Master and his lady at the first two types of events, but at the Ladies' Evening your primary responsibility is to look after the lady on her night. She will be making the response to the one toast of the night that requires it, and you should endeavour to assist in making what might be a nerve-wracking time for her as comfortable as possible.

The Master and his lady may have greeted everyone on arrival in the function room, perhaps with formal introductions by you, and sometimes a photographer will take pictures to record the couples or groups. With modern technology the pictures can be on show after the meal if people wish to keep a souvenir of the evening. Once you have formally escorted the guests of honour to their places at the head of the top table and the meal has started, the Master and his lady will take wine with a series of guests, inserting some of their own requests in addition to the standard lodge wine-taking list.

When the meal is completed there may be presents to distribute to the ladies, and you will have organised table stewards to collect and give out the presents on their table. The Junior Warden or another member will then be called on by you to propose the toast to the ladies, which will hopefully mention the support given to the Master by his lady in his year of office. The proposer may already have indicated to the Master the content of his speech, in case his lady wishes to include some comments about the proposition of the toast. The proposer may also present to the lady any gift that the lodge has collected for as a more enduring mark of appreciation for her work during the year, together with perhaps a bouquet of flowers if this has not been presented to her earlier.

The brother or brethren singing the ladies' song should require no introduction before they perform, although you may feel the need to call for silence before they begin. You announce the Master's lady is eager to reply, and whether or not this is quite the case she will stand to deliver her speech; and you remain behind her ready to ease her chair forward when she sits down again. During her speech she may wish to present some personal gifts of her own, perhaps to the Social Secretary and his lady, who will have been working very hard on their own or with a small committee to ensure that all aspects of a large function have been planned down to the last detail. You will have those gifts and perhaps bouquets of flowers ready to pass to the Master's lady at the appropriate times, and possibly also table prizes to give out if your lodge includes those as well.

You can then escort the Master and his lady out of the function room at the end of the meal, perhaps after you have informed the guests if they need to vacate the room for a short time while it is re-arranged for dancing and less formal seating. You may escort the principal couple onto the dance floor for them to start the first dance. The rest of the evening should continue without any intervention by you, unless the Master and his lady wish to say a few final words at the end of the evening, when you may need to form a circle of guests around the Master, his lady and probably their family to hear those closing comments. All in all a long but hopefully satisfying evening for all of the ladies of the lodge, and especially for the principal lady on her night.

Retirement and the Assistant Director of Ceremonies

After a possibly long and hopefully enjoyable tour of duty as Director of Ceremonies, you hand over to your successor. There is no fixed retirement date for the post, but some lodges like to change their Officers at least every five or so years because they want other members to try their hand at the different jobs, and it is recommended that if possible no tenure of office should exceed 7-10 years. Other lodges, once they have found a capable and willing volunteer and no others have appeared on the horizon, will allow him to continue as long as he wants, and he may eventually find it difficult to hand over if he has held the office for decades.

It is always useful to have a capable ADC working with you, especially when nearing your hand-over to a successor. Although some lodges make the Assistant Secretary a progressive office for juniors, very few will countenance a junior becoming an ADC, so this member is usually a successor in waiting. You may begin placing more of the workload on his shoulders leading up to the hand-over, and let him become accustomed to running affairs under your supervision. He will benefit if you can provide him with copies of the notes you have made for various occasions as the basis of his own checklists, and you will probably be explaining in greater detail the things that by now have become almost second nature to you.

As stated previously, you may always have shared the workload with your ADC, perhaps letting him lead the salutations to Provincial Officers, escorting all latecomers or perhaps those who are not Grand or Provincial Grand Officers, placing and removing the kneeling stool, leading or organising the retiring procession at the end of the meeting. Some of the lodge practices, especially if your lodge has two before each meeting, you can delegate him to organise, perhaps putting the juniors through their paces less formally as they gain confidence. You may also have worked as a team at the installation meetings, with you collecting the people and him the items they will be presented with. In the year before hand-over, you may agree to delegate virtually all of the running of the lodge to him so that he has several dry runs at leading operations, and of course if you have missed a lodge meeting he will have taken over your role on that occasion. Together you may also discuss who would be suitable to replace him as ADC when he steps up, because you both will have enjoyed working as an efficient team, and he will now require the same support as he gave to you.

Probably the most difficult job will be to sit and watch your successor in your shoes, so applaud him when he does well, and only volunteer advice when he asks – everyone has his own way of operating, and you will doubtless have brought your personality into the job when you started. So there may be slight differences, and some of the new ways may even prove to be better suited to the changing requirements of the lodge; all lodges have developed over the years as they have matured, and things that have historically resisted any change have usually ended up like the dinosaurs – extinct.

It is a demanding but very rewarding job, and hopefully you will be remembered among the best Directors of Ceremonies in the lodge. And as a last piece of advice for your successor, which probably stood you in good stead during your term of office:

"Remember that it's nice to be important, but it's more important to be nice."

Appendices

What Each Officer Needs to Know (from the DC)

Tyler

His place in any lodge procession;

How to inform the catering staff of dining numbers as soon as they are reported from the lodge room;

How to report the arrival of dignitaries or latecomers;

How to report the Junior Warden or Director of Ceremonies returning into the lodge room having left to prove the latecomer;

The preparation of the candidates is given in the ritual of the next degree ceremony, except the third which involves everything – use the book or printed lodge advice as an *aide mémoire* if necessary;

Keep the candidate calm by talking to him, explaining the reasons for the preparation if possible;

The knocks on the lodge door may be Emulation or a specific lodge variation;

If not sure about the words of the Tyler from memory, use the book or prompt sheet when the candidate enters the lodge – it sets the scene for the whole ceremony, added to which the Inner Guard repeats almost exactly what the Tyler says, and any variation from the accepted words will make the Inner Guard question his own memory, and any problem of hestitation, etc, may become contagious;

Ensure the re-dressing is as quick as possible – the rest of the lodge is in animated suspense until the candidate's return, although they may be receiving the Almoner's report and other items during the pause;

Ensure that the candidate has practised his salutes before his return, to give him added confidence in lodge;

When to enter and join in any retiring procession;

The Tyler's toast if required at the festive board, and where it should be delivered from (where he is sitting, at the end of the table, behind the Master, etc.).

Inner Guard

His place in any lodge processions;

His responses and salute to the Master's questions during the opening;

His responses and relevant salutes to the Junior Warden when opening the lodge into the higher degrees and closing down;

The correct introductions for latecomers, dignitaries and candidates;

The colloquies with the Tyler and Junior Warden/Master when candidates enter or re-enter the lodge room, and also the actions and when to perform them;

To wait for the Deacons to escort candidates, and possibly the Director of Ceremonies or ADC to escort latecomers and dignitaries;

When to pass forward any implement the Master may require during the ceremony;

The layout of the lighting switches if changes are required in the lodge room during the ceremonies;

How the door locks are operated, and when to open one or both doors for individuals or processions to enter or leave.

Deacons

Their places in opening and closing processions;

Their responses to the Master's questions during opening, if required;

Any formal opening of the Book, lighting and extinguishing candles, etc., during the opening and closing;

How to deliver the Minute Book for signature;

How to conduct ballots, both by paper and balls;

How to escort dignitaries when required;

How to escort candidates around the lodge room;

The answers to the test questions when required;

How to demonstrate advancing to the East;

Where to place the candidate for the entrustings and explanations;

How to inform the candidate appropriately to leave and enter the lodge room;

Where to sit the candidate when the ceremony is over.

Wardens

Their places in the opening and closing processions, as they may precede the Master in the first and follow him in the second;

Their parts in the opening and closing of all three degrees, and whether the closing will be in full or by virtue;

How to announce visitors, dignitaries and latecomers;

How to prove visitors in the three degrees, as appropriate for the lodge meeting;

How the results of ballots are announced, and where to be and when, if appropriate;

What propositions they are expected to make or second (such as the formal acceptance of the Secretary's minutes, the Treasurer's accounts, etc.) and the correct words to be used;

Their roles in the ceremonies, especially when leaving their pedestals in the third degree and the actions they will undertake immediately afterwards

When to follow the Master's gavel and when not, and whether or not they rise with the Master or follow in turn;

What toasts they are to propose at the festive board, and who the responders will be.

Master

Does he personally greet visitors going into the lodge room or after leaving;

What words are needed when welcoming brethren and opening the lodge;

When and how to offer the gavel of the lodge to the representative;

How to submit the minutes for confirmation, with or without the Wardens' proposing and seconding, and how to tell the Secretary his minutes are confirmed;

When to request a visiting dignitary or representative to countersign the minutes;

What words of congratulations to use to welcome joining members and candidates formally into what is now their lodge;

How to announce the risings, seated or standing;

With whom can he take wine without it becoming out of hand;

How to pronounce the items on the formal toast list, and especially what do the initials stand for and which need to be read out loud;

With what words to close the festive board after the Tyler's toast.

Preparation of the Lodge Room

Primarily for the Tyler and Director of Ceremonies; your lodge layout may contain:

Officers' Places:
Master's pedestal – has cushion, closed Book (with bookmarks), square and compasses, gavel, gauntlets, heavy maul and summons in place.
Senior Warden's pedestal – has cushion, Doric column – horizontal, gavel, gauntlets, level, summons.
Junior Warden's pedestal – has cushion, Corinthian column – vertical, gavel, gauntlets, plumb rule, summons.
Deacons, Director of Ceremonies and ADC's seats – the correct holders for the respective wands in place (they may be of different diameters), and also the wands if appropriate.
Inner Guard's seat – has poignard, and square or compasses as appropriate, for use during the entry of the candidates.
Secretary's and Treasurer's table – spare summonses, lodge items, collection plates or bags, Minute Book, pedestal for reading, lodge bylaws, Book of Constitutions for reading of an ancient charge (if required) and regulations for the Master Elect at an installation, lodge ritual for reference, lodge memorabilia, etc.
Tyler's seat – has sword and summons, attendance register or sheet on a table adjacent to the entrance door, and clothing for the candidate if required.

Other Regular Items:
Ancient Charge or Book of Constitutions placed for whoever is reading an ancient charge during the opening of the meeting.
Ashlars to be placed appropriately; the rough one with the Junior Warden or in the North East corner of the square pavement; the perfect ashlar with the Senior Warden or in the South East corner, and the latter ashlar may be mounted on a tripod.
Banner displayed in lodge room near the Master's pedestal.
Candles to be checked they will light, with matches, taper or electricity as appropriate; place matches and taper ready for use (some lodge begin with candles already lit, others have a short ceremony to light them); if electric candles, check they are plugged in and work.
Hymn sheets on all seats or by entrance door (the Secretary, Treasurer and Organist will usually look after their own paperwork).
Officers' collars and aprons on appropriate seats or in the anteroom.

Pointer placed close by the tracing board to be explained, if required.

Tracing boards, if movable, placed appropriately round room and, even if nested together, ensure they are in the correct order.

Visitor cards will assist the Inner Guard announce visitors and latecomers if the need arises; should be with the Tyler's book or signing-in sheets.

Wands to be placed in appropriate stands, or by the door of the lodge if it is customary to process in; doves, Mercuries or sun/moon for the Deacons and crossed wands for the DC and ADC (in some lodges the DC has a baton).

Warrant (check it is correct) displayed in lodge room, or in a pouch for the Master .

Working tools placed appropriately for presentation.

Other features:

Ballot box and balls – placed on Secretary's table if there is a ballot; paper slips if there is to be a written election.

Initiation – blindfold, cable tow and slipper near Tyler's seat; declaration book and collection plate at Secretary's table; Entered Apprentice apron at Master's or Senior Warden's pedestal; first degree tools at Master's or Junior Warden's pedestal; Book of Constitutions and lodge bylaws at the Master's pedestal.

Passing – slipper near Tyler's seat; square at Inner Guard's seat; Fellow Craft apron and second degree tools at Master's or Senior Warden's pedestal.

Raising – two slippers near Tyler's seat; compasses at Inner Guard's seat; floor cloth and emblems of mortality for Deacons to lay out; torch for a Past Master to use; Master Mason apron at Master's or Senior Warden's pedestal (previously check for fit on candidate); third degree tools at Master's pedestal.

Installation – all sets of working tools and list of new Officers at Master's pedestal; Book of Constitutions and lodge bylaws at Secretary's table or appropriately placed; hanger or horse for Officers' collars when handed in; all collars to be worn or in the lodge room ready for investiture (covers absent brethren).

Lectern – in position or ready to be moved into position if there is to be a lecture; often a job for the ADC, Deacons or Inner Guard.

Memorabilia – there may be items donated to the lodge by members or visitors that are to be displayed at meetings, for example on the Secretary's table, as well as other lodge furniture such as gongs, etc.

Mourning – pedestals and Secretary's table draped appropriately; black bows on columns and wands; black rosettes on Officers' collars and for other lodge members; a period of mourning may be decreed by Grand Lodge or Provincial Grand Lodge, or it may be caused by the death of a lodge member.

Ordering meals – count up the number of signatures in the Tyler's book, and check if the Director of Ceremonies has included the initiate(s) if it is a first degree ceremony.

Other Tyler's items – can include sticking plasters (to cover rings and earrings), stout rubber bands (in case the candidate's feet are much smaller than the slipshod), a torch if required in one of the ceremonies (and for power cuts), lighter or matches for the candles, as well as spare white gloves and black tie in case any visitor, and member, has forgotten these items.

Processions In/Out of the Lodge Room

If your lodge has a formal method of conducting the Master and his Wardens to their respective positions in the lodge room, the incoming procession may well include:

Assistant Director of Ceremonies		Director of Ceremonies
Tyler		Inner Guard
Junior Deacon		Senior Deacon
	Other dignitaries as the lodge traditions decree	
Junior Warden		Senior Warden
	Master	
Chaplain		Immediate Past Master

It is noteworthy that the senior of two lodge Officers is on the right-hand side of any pairing, and is therefore walking closest to the centre of the pavement, and this is a general principle adopted in most lodges. If your lodge invites visiting Masters and Provincial Grand Officers to join the inward procession, they will normally fit in behind the Director of Ceremonies or the Deacons, and then everyone stops and turns inwards to form a guard of honour for the Master to pass through into his chair. These additional members of the procession may be in order of seniority, juniors first, and they will find their seats around the East of the lodge room after the Master has taken his place. The Immediate Past Master and Chaplain will also stay in the East, leaving the remaining lodge Officers to escort the Wardens to their positions. The Junior Deacon will step into his place once the Junior Warden has arrived at his pedestal, the Tyler and Inner Guard will peel off to the door if that is situated in the North West, and the Senior Deacon will follow the Director of Ceremonies and his Assistant to his seat in the North East near to the Master.

The retiring procession is almost the same, except that the Assistant Director of Ceremonies stands alone at the front while the Director of Ceremonies is escorting the various brethren to their places in the procession, and he may remain in the lodge room as the procession exits. The Wardens will also follow rather than precede the Master, as they are not forming a guard of honour as the junior Officers will do. Some lodges insist on placing every brother according to rank, while others invite selected brethren only, such as the representative at a meeting, the speaker, Grand Officers, visiting Masters (especially if a lodge is making a formal visit), and possibly the initiate, but each has its own traditions. The Deacons may cross their wands for brethren to pass underneath at both the incoming (Master and Wardens into their pedestals) and outgoing processions and as the Wardens are escorted to their pedestals, whereas the Tyler and Inner Guard will find it more difficult to do so with their standard accoutrements.

124

Formal Seating Plan for Meals

If there is a top table, the Master is seated centrally; next to him on his right hand are:

Initiate;
Provincial Grand Master or his representative;
Grand Officers in descending order of seniority (by year of appointment);
Senior guests.

And on his left hand are:

Immediate Past Master;
Chaplain;
Treasurer;
Secretary;
Director of Ceremonies;
Past Masters of the lodge in order of seniority.

The Wardens may be seated at the ends of the top table, or at the ends of the outermost sprig tables, depending on lodge custom and practice.

The Master's personal guests may be seated in front of him on an adjacent sprig table, so that he has the opportunity to converse with them during the meal.

If there is music or the Master's song is to be sung during or after the meal, it is likely that the brethren involved will want to sit together, to make any last minute musical arrangements, and the pianist will probably prefer to be seated near to the piano.

Some senior attendees, which may include Grand Officers (sometimes referred to as Officers of Grand Lodge, but please not Grand Lodge Officers), may request to be seated elsewhere in the table plan, perhaps to be near other guests who cannot be placed adjacent to the top table for them to converse with. You might even invite them to consider doing this occasionally, so that they can mix with the other ranks of Masons present; it has a remarkably encouraging effect if junior brethren realise they are sitting and talking with senior brethren, and each can usefully learn informally from the other, which they might not otherwise be able to do if the seating plans always follow a strict hierarchical order.

Taking Wine and Formal Toasts

Taking Wine

The taking of wine with the brethren can be fraught with difficulties. Too little will leave some attendees feeling overlooked, and too much of a good thing will potentially spoil the proceedings for everyone. It is unnecessary to interrupt every course of the meal by taking wine, so try to complete the necessary items in perhaps one or two sessions, and then the diners can continue their meals in peace.

As a way of introducing some variety into your preamble to take wine, you may say that the Master: now wishes, has expressed the wish/desire,
will take great/particular pleasure,
is delighted and honoured, is equally delighted,
is now eager/anxious, is now proud and happy.

The following list may be of assistance to the Master as he takes wine with the:

Wardens (particularly if they join in with the Master in subsequent toasts)
Provincial Grand Master or representative (he may then take wine with everyone else)
Grand Officers
Provincial Grand Officers
Visiting Masters
A brother on a special celebration, e.g. 50th anniversary
Officers and members of the lodge who participated in the ceremony
Candidate (new Initiate, Fellowcraft, Master Mason)
Joining members
Master Elect
New lodge Officers
Founders or Past Masters of the lodge
Personal guests
Other (or all) members of the lodge
Other (or all) visiting brethren
Any brother with whom he has not yet taken wine (an alternative catch-all)

Toasts

The following is a generally accepted set of toasts to be used on formal occasions:

Monarch (and the Craft)

MW Grand Master

MW Pro Grand Master
RW Deputy Grand Master
RW Assistant Grand Master
And the rest of the Grand Officers, present and past

RW Provincial Grand Master

Deputy Provincial Grand Master
Assistant Provincial Grand Master(s)
And the rest of the Provincial Grand Officers, present and past, of this and other Provinces, and holders of Metropolitan (Grand) Rank

Master

Immediate Past (and Installing) Master

Installation team

Masonic charities

Absent brethren (if referred to as the 9 o'clock toast – when the hands of the clock are at the square – it should be honoured at 9pm; if designated to absent brethren, this can be taken at any time)

Founders of the lodge

Visiting brethren

Tyler's toast (may be the long version at an installation, Olde English Night)

The charity collection, taken in lodge or at the festive board, may be announced by the Master before or during his closing remarks. If the lodge responds to the toasts using firing glasses, then there is usually no fire after absent brethren if it precedes the loyal toast (which preferably it does not), after Masonic charities, or after the Tyler's toast, or there may be "silent fire". Some lodges adopt "silent fire" and others deprecate it, but your visitors should be courteous and "when in Rome…"

Serenity for Directors of Ceremonies

Grant me the serenity to accept the things I cannot change;
    the courage to change the things I cannot accept;
        and the wisdom to hide the bodies of those I had to kill today,
            because they got on my nerves.

Also help me to be careful of the toes I step on today,
    as they may be connected to the feet I have to kiss tomorrow.

And help me to remember that when I am having a bad day,
    and it seems that people are trying to wind me up,
        it takes 42 muscles to frown,
            but only 28 to smile.

Acknowledgements

I would like to thank the several lodges that allowed me to browse through their minute books and to select the different sets of minutes as examples in this book. I would like to express my appreciation for the constructive comments on the text made by Chris Godden of Nourse Lodge 8590, and Norman Thompson of Huddleston Lodge 6041 and Albert Cherry of Brigantes Lodge 9734 for proof reading different parts of the book; as well as placing on record – as ever – the patience of my wife Linda while I was immersed in researching for and compiling this book.

The printing royalties from this book will be given to the Cumberland & Westmorland 2007 Festival for the Royal Masonic Trust for Girls and Boys